Gates of Prayer for Weekdays

תפלות ליום חול

A Gender-Sensitive Prayerbook

Chaim Stern, Editor

CENTRAL CONFERENCE OF AMERICAN RABBIS
1993

On Usage

The following typographic conventions are used in this prayerbook. They are suggestions only, and congregations should feel free to follow their own *minhagim*.

The roman typestyle is used whenever we suggest the English be read by the person leading the service.

> *Paragraphs set in italics and indented might be read in English by the congregation as a whole. In congregations where unison reading is not the norm, such passages may be read by diverse individuals.*

Smaller roman type is used for passages which might be chanted or sung—generally in Hebrew.

San serif type is used for transliterations.

° The open circle signifies that the English is a variation on the theme of—rather than a translation of—the Hebrew.

■ The solid box is used for footnotes.

* Asterisks mark insertions for special occasions.

_ indicates a *kamatz katan*, pronounced like the *o* in "often".

Designed by Barry Nostradamus Sher. Composed at Nostradamus Advertising by Warren Wolfsohn. Hebrew set in NewHebrew, developed by Warren Wolfsohn from Hadassah (Davka Corporation) and Hebraica (Linguist's Software, Inc.). Copyediting by Dr. Yehiel Hayon.

CCAR Press, 192 Lexington Av., New York, NY 10016   (212) 684-4990
Printed in the United States of America.
99 98 97 96 95 94 93   10 9 8 7 6 5 4 3 2 1

ISBN:
0-88123-040-5 *(Heb. opening)*
0-88123-038-3 *(Eng. opening)*

Contents

Preface

Just before *Gates of Prayer* went to press in late 1974, the editor changed all English-language references to human beings in general that on their face excluded women, to gender-neutral terms. Thus, 'mankind' became 'humankind,' 'fathers' became 'ancestors' or 'fathers and mothers,' and so on. He did not at that time change language referring to God and he made no attempt to emend the Hebrew texts. Now, sixteen years later, we present several services for Shabbat in which the gender-neutral approach is extended to English-language references to God, and, in some small degree, to the Hebrew.

There are few tasks in liturgy more challenging than the one currently under discussion in the Reform movement and in other branches of Judaism, both in North America and elsewhere: how to respond to the need, felt by many, to reshape the language of our liturgy so that it will reflect our view that masculine language and exclusively male assumptions ought to give way to more inclusive expression.

We hope the present volume may be a contribution toward that end.

We thank the many colleagues whose helpful suggestions and criticisms have been gratefully received and carefully considered. This edition would have been the poorer without their help. Rabbi H. Leonard Poller, Rabbi Donna Berman, and Cantor Edward Graham formed, with the editor, a working group that studied the editor's final draft, and helped decide on many matters. To them, a particular word of thanks.

Chaim Stern
CHAPPAQUA, NEW YORK

Meditations and Readings for Worship
הגיונות

❧ 1

THE REBBE of Tsanz was asked by a Chasid: What does the
Rabbi do before praying? I pray, was the reply, that I may be
able to pray properly.

❧ 2

I HAVE always found prayer difficult. So often it seems like a
fruitless game of hide-and-seek where we seek and God
hides. . . . Yet I cannot leave prayer alone for long. My need
drives me to God. And I have a feeling . . . that finally all my
seeking will prove infinitely worthwhile. And I am not sure
what I mean by 'finding'. Some days my very seeking seems a
kind of 'finding'. And, of course, if 'finding' means the *end* of
'seeking', it were better to go on seeking.

❧ 3

CONSIDER how high God is above the world! Yet if one enters
the synagogue and stands behind a pillar and prays in a whisper,
the Holy One, the Blessed One, listens to that prayer. . . . Can
there be a God nearer than this, who is as near to God's
creatures as the mouth is to the ear?

❧ 4

I DO NOT pretend to understand how the divine Creator
influences the human child. I feel as if spiritual forces were
pouring constantly from the infinite source which is never
poorer for all it gives forth. . . . Yet the influences of spirit make
their way in different degrees, or not at all, to different souls.

The windows of some are perhaps nearly shut. The windows of others have open only a few chinks and crevices. At some seasons—the seasons of prayer—those chinks and crevices may open a little wider so that a little more of God's light may enter in.

❧ 5

TRUE PRAYER is the opening of our hearts Godward, and the answer is a flow of light and influence from God.

Prayer means a consciousness full of God's presence and of our relation with the Divine.

God's aim is the increase of spiritual and moral goodness in the world, to lead the universe toward perfection. God's laws are in their workings organized toward this end. Those who are loyal to God must organize their own lives to be within the sphere of the workings of these laws.

❧ 6

PRAYER gives us the guidance we need. It opens the mind to the illumination of God. The prophets made their whole life an act of prayer—so they received the inspiration of God. Our humbler minds, standing much below the heights in which they stood, receiving for the most part only a reflected illumination, may now and then, by climbing a little higher, catch a glimpse of the direct light. Through prayer, we can receive the guidance of God to strengthen our hold on truth, goodness, righteousness and purity, which are the laws for humanity emanating from the nature of God.

❧ 7

CHIEF among the duties of the heart is the attuning of the soul into such perfect harmony with God that all right conduct and right thought must follow without effort on our part, because our will is one with God's, through love.

 る 8

PRAYER is speech, but not 'mere' speech. The word is not to be despised. Words have power over the soul. "Hear, O Israel!" is a cry and an affirmation, a reminder of glory and martyrdom, a part of the very essence of our people's history. Our prayer-books are but words on paper; they can mean little or nothing. Yet the searching spirit and questing heart may find great power in their words. Through them we link ourselves to all the generations of our people, pouring out our souls in prayer with those of our brothers and sisters. These words, laden with the tears and joys of centuries, have the power to bring us into the very presence of God. Not easily, not all at once, not every time, but somehow, sometimes, the worshipper who offers up heart and mind without reservation will know that she has touched the Throne of Glory.

る 9

I REGARD the old Jewish *Siddur* as the most important single Jewish book—a more personal expression, a closer record, of Jewish sufferings, Jewish needs, Jewish hopes and aspirations, than the Bible itself. For one thing the Bible is too grand and universal to be exclusively Jewish (as Shakespeare is not the typical Englishman), and for another, whatever is quintessentially needed for daily use has been squeezed out of it into the prayerbook and so made our daily own. And if you want to know what Judaism is—the question which has no answer if debated on the plane of intellectual argument—you can find it by absorbing that book. The Jewish soul is mirrored there as nowhere else, mirrored or rather embodied there: the individual's soul in his private sorrows, and the people's soul in its historic burdens, its heroic passion and suffering, its unfaltering faith, through the ages.

Evening Service   ערבית לחול

The synagogue is the sanctuary of Israel. Born of our longing for the living God, it has been to Israel, throughout our wanderings, a visible token of the presence of God in our people's midst. Its beauty is the beauty of holiness; steadfast it has stood as the champion of justice, mercy, and peace.

> *Its truths are true for all people. Its love is a love for all people. Its God is the God of all people, as it has been said: "My house shall be called a house of prayer for all peoples."*

Let all the family of Israel, all who hunger for righteousness, all who seek the Eternal, find God here—and here find life!

OR

Praise the Everlasting God in the dark of night
and in the light of day.
> *Praised be the One whose glory fills heaven and earth.*

Praise the One who made this green earth our dwelling place.
> *Praised be the One whose love is the breath of our life.*

From generation to generation we give thanks to Your name;
> *to the end of time we will sing Your praise.*

All rise

The Sh'ma and Its Blessings שמע וברכותיה

בָּרְכוּ אֶת־יי הַמְבֹרָךְ!

Praise the One to whom our praise is due!

בָּרוּךְ יי הַמְבֹרָךְ לְעוֹלָם וָעֶד!

Ba-ruch Adonai ha-m'vo-rach l'o-lam va-ed!

Praised be the One to whom our praise is due, now and for ever!

CREATION מעריב ערבים

בָּרוּךְ אַתָּה יי, אֱלֹהֵינוּ מֶלֶךְ הָעוֹלָם, אֲשֶׁר בִּדְבָרוֹ
מַעֲרִיב עֲרָבִים, בְּחָכְמָה פּוֹתֵחַ שְׁעָרִים, וּבִתְבוּנָה מְשַׁנֶּה
עִתִּים, וּמַחֲלִיף אֶת־הַזְּמַנִּים, וּמְסַדֵּר אֶת־הַכּוֹכָבִים
בְּמִשְׁמְרוֹתֵיהֶם בָּרָקִיעַ כִּרְצוֹנוֹ.

בּוֹרֵא יוֹם וָלַיְלָה, גּוֹלֵל אוֹר מִפְּנֵי חֹשֶׁךְ וְחֹשֶׁךְ מִפְּנֵי אוֹר,
וּמַעֲבִיר יוֹם וּמֵבִיא לָיְלָה, וּמַבְדִּיל בֵּין יוֹם וּבֵין לָיְלָה,
יי צְבָאוֹת שְׁמוֹ. אֵל חַי וְקַיָּם, תָּמִיד יִמְלוֹךְ עָלֵינוּ,
לְעוֹלָם וָעֶד. בָּרוּךְ אַתָּה יי, הַמַּעֲרִיב עֲרָבִים.

Praised be our Eternal God, Ruler of the universe, whose word brings on the evening, whose wisdom opens heaven's gates, whose understanding makes the ages pass and the seasons alternate, and whose will controls the stars as they travel through the skies.

You are Creator of day and night, rolling light away from darkness, and darkness from light; You cause day to pass and bring on the night; separating day from night; You command the Hosts of Heaven! May the living and eternal God rule us always, to the end of time! We praise You, Eternal One, whose word makes evening fall.

5

REVELATION   אהבת עולם

אַהֲבַת עוֹלָם בֵּית יִשְׂרָאֵל עַמְּךָ אָהָבְתָּ.
תּוֹרָה וּמִצְוֹת, חֻקִּים וּמִשְׁפָּטִים אוֹתָנוּ לִמַּדְתָּ.

עַל־כֵּן, יי אֱלֹהֵינוּ, בְּשָׁכְבֵּנוּ וּבְקוּמֵנוּ נָשִׂיחַ בְּחֻקֶּיךָ,
וְנִשְׂמַח בְּדִבְרֵי תוֹרָתֶךָ וּבְמִצְוֹתֶיךָ לְעוֹלָם וָעֶד.

כִּי הֵם חַיֵּינוּ וְאֹרֶךְ יָמֵינוּ, וּבָהֶם נֶהְגֶּה יוֹמָם וָלָיְלָה.
וְאַהֲבָתְךָ אַל־תָּסוּר מִמֶּנּוּ לְעוֹלָמִים!
בָּרוּךְ אַתָּה יי, אוֹהֵב עַמּוֹ יִשְׂרָאֵל.

Unending is Your love for Your people, the House of Israel:
Torah and Mitzvot, laws and precepts have You taught us.

Therefore, O God, when we lie down and when we rise up, we
will meditate on Your laws and rejoice in Your Torah and
Mitzvot for ever.

*Day and night we will reflect on them, for they are our
life and the length of our days. Then Your love shall
never depart from our hearts! We praise You, Eternal
One: You love Your people Israel.*

❖ ❖

שְׁמַע יִשְׂרָאֵל: יהוה אֱלֹהֵינוּ, יהוה אֶחָד!

Sh'ma Yis-ra-eil: Adonai Eh-lo-hei-nu, Adonai Eh-chad!

Hear, O Israel: the Eternal One is our God,
the Eternal God alone!

בָּרוּךְ שֵׁם כְּבוֹד מַלְכוּתוֹ לְעוֹלָם וָעֶד!

Ba-ruch sheim k'vod mal-chu-toh l'o-lam va-ed!

Blessed is God's glorious majesty for ever and ever!

All are seated

6

וְאָהַבְתָּ אֵת יְהוָה אֱלֹהֶיךָ בְּכָל־לְבָבְךָ וּבְכָל־נַפְשְׁךָ
וּבְכָל־מְאֹדֶךָ: וְהָיוּ הַדְּבָרִים הָאֵלֶּה אֲשֶׁר אָנֹכִי מְצַוְּךָ
הַיּוֹם עַל־לְבָבֶךָ: וְשִׁנַּנְתָּם לְבָנֶיךָ וְדִבַּרְתָּ בָּם בְּשִׁבְתְּךָ
בְּבֵיתֶךָ וּבְלֶכְתְּךָ בַדֶּרֶךְ וּבְשָׁכְבְּךָ וּבְקוּמֶךָ: וּקְשַׁרְתָּם
לְאוֹת עַל־יָדֶךָ וְהָיוּ לְטֹטָפֹת בֵּין עֵינֶיךָ: וּכְתַבְתָּם
עַל־מְזוּזֹת בֵּיתֶךָ וּבִשְׁעָרֶיךָ:

V'a-hav-ta et Adonai Eh-lo-heh-cha b'chol l'va-v'cha u-v'chol naf-sh'cha u-v'chol m'o-deh-cha. V'ha-yu ha-d'va-rim ha-ei-leh a-sher a-no-chi m'tza-v'cha ha-yom al l'va-veh-cha. V'shi-nan-tam l'va-neh-cha v'di-bar-ta bam b'shiv-t'cha b'vei-teh-cha u-v'lech-t'cha va-deh-rech u-v'shoch-b'cha u-v'ku-meh-cha. U-k'shar-tam l'oht al ya-deh-cha v'ha-yu l'toh-ta-foht bein ei-neh-cha; u-ch'tav-tam al m'zu-zoht bei-teh-cha u-vi-sh'a-reh-cha.

You shall love the Eternal One, your God, with all your heart, with all your mind, with all your being. Set these words, which I command you this day, upon your heart. Teach them faithfully to your children; speak of them in your home and on your way, when you lie down and when you rise up. Bind them as a sign upon your hand; let them be a symbol before your eyes; inscribe them on the door-posts of your house, and on your gates.

לְמַעַן תִּזְכְּרוּ וַעֲשִׂיתֶם אֶת־כָּל־מִצְוֹתָי וִהְיִיתֶם קְדֹשִׁים
לֵאלֹהֵיכֶם: אֲנִי יְהוָה אֱלֹהֵיכֶם אֲשֶׁר הוֹצֵאתִי אֶתְכֶם
מֵאֶרֶץ מִצְרַיִם לִהְיוֹת לָכֶם לֵאלֹהִים אֲנִי יְהוָה אֱלֹהֵיכֶם:

L'ma-an tiz-k'ru va-a-si-tem et kol mitz-vo-tai, vi-h'yi-tem k'doh-shim lei-lo-hei-chem. A-ni Adonai Eh-lo-hei-chem a-sher ho-tzei-ti et-chem mei-eh-retz mitz-ra-yim li-h'yoht la-chem lei-lo-him. A-ni Adonai Eh-lo-hei-chem.

Be mindful of all My Mitzvot, and do them: so shall you consecrate yourselves to your God. I am your Eternal God who led you out of Egypt to be your God; I am your Eternal God.

REDEMPTION   גאולה

אֱמֶת וֶאֱמוּנָה כָּל־זֹאת, וְקַיָּם עָלֵינוּ כִּי הוּא יי אֱלֹהֵינוּ
וְאֵין זוּלָתוֹ, וַאֲנַחְנוּ יִשְׂרָאֵל עַמּוֹ. הַפּוֹדֵנוּ מִיַּד מְלָכִים,
מַלְכֵּנוּ הַגּוֹאֲלֵנוּ מִכַּף כָּל־הֶעָרִיצִים.
הָעֹשֶׂה גְדֹלוֹת עַד אֵין חֵקֶר, וְנִפְלָאוֹת עַד־אֵין מִסְפָּר.
הַשָּׂם נַפְשֵׁנוּ בַּחַיִּים, וְלֹא־נָתַן לַמּוֹט רַגְלֵנוּ.
הָעֹשֶׂה לָּנוּ נִסִּים בְּפַרְעֹה, אוֹתוֹת וּמוֹפְתִים בְּאַדְמַת
בְּנֵי חָם. וַיּוֹצֵא אֶת־עַמּוֹ יִשְׂרָאֵל מִתּוֹכָם לְחֵרוּת עוֹלָם.
וְרָאוּ בָנָיו וּבְנוֹתָיו גְּבוּרָתוֹ; שִׁבְּחוּ וְהוֹדוּ לִשְׁמוֹ.
וּמַלְכוּתוֹ בְּרָצוֹן קִבְּלוּ עֲלֵיהֶם. מֹשֶׁה וּמִרְיָם וּבְנֵי
יִשְׂרָאֵל לְךָ עָנוּ שִׁירָה בְּשִׂמְחָה רַבָּה, וְאָמְרוּ כֻלָּם:

All this we hold to be true and sure; You alone are our God;
there is none else, and we are Israel Your people.

> *You are our Sovereign: You deliver us from the hand of*
> *oppressors, and save us from the fist of tyrants.*

You do wonders without number,
marvels that pass our understanding.

> *You give us our life; by Your help we survive all*
> *who seek our destruction.*

You did wonders for us in the land of Egypt,
miracles and marvels in the land of Pharaoh.

> *You led Your people Israel out,*
> *forever to serve You in freedom.*

When Your children witnessed Your power, they extolled You
and gave You thanks; willingly they enthroned You; and, full of
joy, Moses, Miriam, and all Israel sang this song:

מִי־כָמְכָה בָּאֵלִם, יהוה? מִי כָּמְכָה, נֶאְדָּר בַּקֹּדֶשׁ,
נוֹרָא תְהִלֹּת, עֹשֵׂה פֶלֶא?

מַלְכוּתְךָ רָאוּ בָנֶיךָ, בּוֹקֵעַ יָם לִפְנֵי מֹשֶׁה; זֶה אֵלִי!
עָנוּ וְאָמְרוּ: יהוה יִמְלֹךְ לְעֹלָם וָעֶד!

וְנֶאֱמַר: כִּי פָדָה יי אֶת־יַעֲקֹב, וּגְאָלוֹ מִיַּד חָזָק מִמֶּנּוּ.
בָּרוּךְ אַתָּה יי, גָּאַל יִשְׂרָאֵל.

Mi cha-mo-cha ba-ei-lim, Adonai? Mi ka-mo-cha, neh-dar ba-ko-
desh, no-ra t'hi-loht, o-sei feh-leh?

Mal-chu-t'cha ra-u va-neh-cha, bo-kei-a yam lif-nei Mo-sheh; zeh ei-li!
a-nu v'am-ru: Adonai yim-loch l'o-lam va-ed.

V'neh-eh-mar: Ki fa-da Adonai et Ya-a-kov, u-g'a-lo mi-yad cha-zak
mi-meh-nu. Ba-ruch a-ta Adonai, ga-al Yis-ra-eil.

Who is like You, Eternal One, among the gods that are worshipped?
Who is like You, majestic in holiness, awesome in splendor, doing
wonders?

In their escape from the sea, Your children saw Your sovereign might
displayed. "This is my God!" they cried. "The Eternal will reign
for ever and ever!"

And it has been said: The Eternal One delivered Jacob, and redeemed
us from the hand of one stronger than ourselves. We praise You,
Eternal One, Redeemer of Israel.

DIVINE PROVIDENCE   הַשְׁכִּיבֵנוּ

הַשְׁכִּיבֵנוּ, יי אֱלֹהֵינוּ, לְשָׁלוֹם, וְהַעֲמִידֵנוּ, מַלְכֵּנוּ, לְחַיִּים.
וּפְרוֹשׂ עָלֵינוּ סֻכַּת שְׁלוֹמֶךָ, וְתַקְּנֵנוּ בְּעֵצָה טוֹבָה מִלְּפָנֶיךָ,
וְהוֹשִׁיעֵנוּ לְמַעַן שְׁמֶךָ, וְהָגֵן בַּעֲדֵנוּ. וְהָסֵר מֵעָלֵינוּ אוֹיֵב,
דֶּבֶר וְחֶרֶב וְרָעָב וְיָגוֹן; וְהָסֵר שָׂטָן מִלְּפָנֵינוּ וּמֵאַחֲרֵינוּ,
וּבְצֵל כְּנָפֶיךָ תַּסְתִּירֵנוּ, כִּי אֵל שׁוֹמְרֵנוּ וּמַצִּילֵנוּ אָתָּה,

כִּי אֵל מֶלֶךְ חַנּוּן וְרַחוּם אָתָּה. וּשְׁמוֹר צֵאתֵנוּ וּבוֹאֵנוּ
לְחַיִּים וּלְשָׁלוֹם, מֵעַתָּה וְעַד עוֹלָם.
בָּרוּךְ אַתָּה יי, שׁוֹמֵר עַמּוֹ יִשְׂרָאֵל לָעַד.

Grant that we may lie down in peace, Eternal God, and raise us
up, O Sovereign, to life renewed. Spread over us the shelter of
Your peace; guide us with Your good counsel; and for Your
name's sake, be our Help.

Shield us from hatred and plague; keep us from war and
famine and anguish; subdue our inclination to evil. O God,
our Guardian and Helper, our gracious and merciful Ruler,
give us refuge in the shadow of Your wings. O guard our
coming and our going, that now and always we have life
and peace.

We praise You, Eternal One, the Guardian of Israel.

All rise

READER'S KADDISH   חצי קדיש

יִתְגַּדַּל וְיִתְקַדַּשׁ שְׁמֵהּ רַבָּא בְּעָלְמָא דִּי־בְרָא כִרְעוּתֵהּ,
וְיַמְלִיךְ מַלְכוּתֵהּ בְּחַיֵּיכוֹן וּבְיוֹמֵיכוֹן וּבְחַיֵּי דְכָל־בֵּית
יִשְׂרָאֵל, בַּעֲגָלָא וּבִזְמַן קָרִיב, וְאִמְרוּ: אָמֵן.

יְהֵא שְׁמֵהּ רַבָּא מְבָרַךְ לְעָלַם וּלְעָלְמֵי עָלְמַיָּא.

יִתְבָּרַךְ וְיִשְׁתַּבַּח, וְיִתְפָּאַר וְיִתְרוֹמַם וְיִתְנַשֵּׂא, וְיִתְהַדָּר
וְיִתְעַלֶּה וְיִתְהַלָּל שְׁמֵהּ דְּקוּדְשָׁא, בְּרִיךְ הוּא, לְעֵלָּא
מִן־כָּל־בִּרְכָתָא וְשִׁירָתָא, תֻּשְׁבְּחָתָא וְנֶחֱמָתָא
דַּאֲמִירָן בְּעָלְמָא, וְאִמְרוּ: אָמֵן.

Yit-ga-dal v'yit-ka-dash sh'mei ra-ba b'al-ma di-v'ra chir-u-tei,
v'yam-lich mal-chu-tei b'cha-yei-chon u-v'yo-mei-chon u-v'cha-yei
d'chol beit Yis-ra-eil, ba-a-ga-la u-viz-man ka-riv, v'im'ru: A-mein.

Y'hei sh'mei ra-ba m'va-rach l'a-lam u-l'al-mei al-ma-ya.

Yit-ba-rach v'yish-ta-bach v'yit-pa-ar, v'yit-ro-mam, v'yit-na-sei, v'yit-ha-dar, v'yit-a-leh, v'yit-ha-lal sh'mei d'kud'sha, b'rich hu, l'ei-la min kol bir-cha-ta v'shi-ra-ta, tush-b'cha-ta v'neh-cheh-ma-ta da-a-mi-ran b'al-ma, v'im'ru: A-mein.

Let the glory of God be extolled, and God's great name be hallowed in the world whose creation God willed. May God rule in our own day, in our own lives, and in the life of all Israel, and let us say: Amen.

Let God's great name be praised for ever and ever.

Beyond all the praises, songs, and adorations that we can utter is the Holy One, the Blessed One, whom yet we glorify, honor, and exalt. And let us say: Amen.

תפלה T'filah

אֲדֹנָי, שְׂפָתַי תִּפְתָּח וּפִי יַגִּיד תְּהִלָּתֶךָ.

Eternal God, open my lips, that my mouth may declare Your glory.

GOD OF ALL GENERATIONS   אבות ואמהות

בָּרוּךְ אַתָּה יי, אֱלֹהֵינוּ וֵאלֹהֵי אֲבוֹתֵינוּ וְאִמּוֹתֵינוּ:
אֱלֹהֵי אַבְרָהָם, אֱלֹהֵי יִצְחָק, וֵאלֹהֵי יַעֲקֹב.
אֱלֹהֵי שָׂרָה, אֱלֹהֵי רִבְקָה, אֱלֹהֵי לֵאָה, וֵאלֹהֵי רָחֵל.
הָאֵל הַגָּדוֹל הַגִּבּוֹר וְהַנּוֹרָא, אֵל עֶלְיוֹן, גּוֹמֵל חֲסָדִים
טוֹבִים וְקוֹנֵה הַכֹּל, וְזוֹכֵר חַסְדֵי אָבוֹת וְאִמָּהוֹת,
וּמֵבִיא גְאֻלָּה לִבְנֵי בְנֵיהֶם, לְמַעַן שְׁמוֹ בְּאַהֲבָה.

BETWEEN ROSH HASHANAH AND YOM KIPPUR ADD:

זָכְרֵנוּ לְחַיִּים, מֶלֶךְ חָפֵץ בַּחַיִּים,
וְכָתְבֵנוּ בְּסֵפֶר הַחַיִּים, לְמַעַנְךָ אֱלֹהִים חַיִּים.

מֶלֶךְ עוֹזֵר וּמוֹשִׁיעַ וּמָגֵן.
בָּרוּךְ אַתָּה יי, מָגֵן אַבְרָהָם וְעֶזְרַת שָׂרָה.

Ba-ruch a-ta Adonai, Eh-lo-hei-nu vei-lo-hei a-vo-tei-nu v'i-mo-tei-nu:
Eh-lo-hei Av-ra-ham, Eh-lo-hei Yitz-chak, vei-lo-hei Ya-a-kov. Eh-lo-
hei Sa-rah, Eh-lo-hei Riv-kah, Eh-lo-hei Lei-ah, vei-lo-hei Ra-cheil.
Ha-eil ha-ga-dol ha-gi-bor v'ha-no-ra, Eil el-yon. Go-meil cha-sa-dim
toh-vim, v'ko-nei ha-kol, v'zo-cheir chas-dei a-voht v'i-ma-hoht, u-
mei-vi g'u-la li-v'nei v'nei-hem, l'ma-an sh'mo, b'a-ha-va.

BETWEEN ROSH HASHANAH AND YOM KIPPUR ADD:

Zoch'rei-nu l'cha-yim, meh-lech cha-feitz ba-cha-yim,
v'cho-t'vei-nu b'sei-fer ha-cha-yim, l'ma-an-cha Eh-lo-him cha-yim.

Meh-lech o-zeir u-mo-shi-a u-ma-gein.
Ba-ruch a-ta Adonai, ma-gein Av-ra-ham v'ez-rat Sa-rah.

Praised be our God, the God of our fathers and our mothers: God
of Abraham, God of Isaac, and God of Jacob; God of Sarah, God
of Rebekah, God of Leah and God of Rachel; great, mighty, and
awesome God, God supreme.

Ruler of all the living, Your ways are ways of love. You remember the faithfulness of our ancestors, and in love bring redemption to their children's children for the sake of Your name.

BETWEEN ROSH HASHANAH AND YOM KIPPUR ADD:

Remember us unto life, Sovereign who delights in life, and inscribe
us in the Book of Life, that Your will may prevail, O God of life.

You are our Sovereign and our Help, our Redeemer and our
Shield. We praise You, Eternal One, Shield of Abraham,
Protector of Sarah.

GOD'S POWER   גבורות

אַתָּה גִבּוֹר לְעוֹלָם, אֲדֹנָי, מְחַיֵּה הַכֹּל אַתָּה, רַב לְהוֹשִׁיעַ.
מְכַלְכֵּל חַיִּים בְּחֶסֶד, מְחַיֵּה הַכֹּל בְּרַחֲמִים רַבִּים. סוֹמֵךְ
נוֹפְלִים, וְרוֹפֵא חוֹלִים, וּמַתִּיר אֲסוּרִים, וּמְקַיֵּם אֱמוּנָתוֹ
לִישֵׁנֵי עָפָר. מִי כָמְוֹךָ בַּעַל גְּבוּרוֹת, וּמִי דְוֹמֶה לָּךְ, מֶלֶךְ
מֵמִית וּמְחַיֵּה וּמַצְמִיחַ יְשׁוּעָה?

12

BETWEEN ROSH HASHANAH AND YOM KIPPUR ADD:

מִי כָמְוֹךָ, אֵל הָרַחֲמִים, זוֹכֵר יְצוּרָיו לְחַיִּים בְּרַחֲמִים?

וְנֶאֱמָן אַתָּה לְהַחֲיוֹת הַכֹּל. בָּרוּךְ אַתָּה יי, מְחַיֵּה הַכֹּל.

A-ta gi-bor l'o-lam, Adonai, m'cha-yei ha-kol a-ta, rav l'ho-shi-a.
M'chal-keil cha-yim b'cheh-sed, m'cha-yei ha-kol b'ra-cha-mim ra-
bim. So-meich no-f'lim, v'ro-fei cho-lim, u-ma-tir a-su-rim, u-m'ka-
yeim eh-mu-na-toh li-shei-nei a-far. Mi cha-mo-cha ba-al g'vu-roht,
u-mi doh-meh lach, meh-lech mei-mit u-m'cha-yeh u-matz-mi-ach
y'shu-a?

BETWEEN ROSH HASHANAH AND YOM KIPPUR ADD:

Mi cha-mo-cha, Eil ha-ra-cha-mim, zo-cheir y'tzu-rav l'cha-yim
b'ra-cha-mim?

V'neh-eh-man a-ta l'ha-cha-yoht ha-kol. Ba-ruch a-ta Adonai,
m'cha-yei ha-kol.

*Eternal is Your might, O God; all life is Your gift; great is
Your power to save!*

*With love You sustain the living, with great compassion
give life to all. You send help to the falling and healing to
the sick; You bring freedom to the captive and keep faith
with those who sleep in the dust.*

*Who is like You, Mighty One? Who is Your equal, Author of
life and death, Source of salvation?*

BETWEEN ROSH HASHANAH AND YOM KIPPUR ADD:

Who is like You, Source of mercy?
In compassion You sustain the life of Your children.

We praise You, Eternal God, Source of life.

THE HOLINESS OF GOD · קְדוּשַׁת הַשֵּׁם

אַתָּה קָדוֹשׁ וְשִׁמְךָ קָדוֹשׁ, וּקְדוֹשִׁים בְּכָל־יוֹם יְהַלְלְוּךָ סֶּלָה.
*בָּרוּךְ אַתָּה יי, הָאֵל הַקָּדוֹשׁ.

*BETWEEN ROSH HASHANAH AND YOM KIPPUR CONCLUDE:

בָּרוּךְ אַתָּה יי, הַמֶּלֶךְ הַקָּדוֹשׁ.

You are holy, Your name is holy, and those who strive to be holy
declare Your glory day by day.

*We praise You, Eternal One, the holy God.

*BETWEEN ROSH HASHANAH AND YOM KIPPUR CONCLUDE:

We praise You, Eternal One: You rule in holiness.

All are seated

(The Intermediate Benedictions, through
page 18, may be recited silently.)

WISDOM · בִּינָה

אַתָּה חוֹנֵן לְאָדָם דַּעַת וּמְלַמֵּד לֶאֱנוֹשׁ בִּינָה. חָנֵּנוּ מֵאִתְּךָ
דֵּעָה, בִּינָה וְהַשְׂכֵּל. בָּרוּךְ אַתָּה יי, חוֹנֵן הַדָּעַת.

BY YOUR GRACE we have the power to gain knowledge and to
learn wisdom. Favor us with knowledge, wisdom, and insight,
for You are their Source.

We praise You, Eternal One, gracious Giver of knowledge.

REPENTANCE · תְּשׁוּבָה

הֲשִׁיבֵנוּ אָבִינוּ לְתוֹרָתֶךָ, וְקָרְבֵנוּ מַלְכֵּנוּ לַעֲבוֹדָתֶךָ,
וְהַחֲזִירֵנוּ בִּתְשׁוּבָה שְׁלֵמָה לְפָנֶיךָ. בָּרוּךְ אַתָּה יי,
הָרוֹצֶה בִּתְשׁוּבָה.

14

HELP US, our Creator, to return to Your Teaching; draw us near, our Sovereign, to Your service; and bring us back into Your presence in perfect repentance.

We praise You, Eternal One: You delight in repentance.

FORGIVENESS   סליחה

סְלַח־לָנוּ אָבִינוּ כִּי חָטָאנוּ, מְחַל־לָנוּ מַלְכֵּנוּ כִּי פָשָׁעְנוּ,
כִּי מוֹחֵל וְסוֹלֵחַ אָתָּה. בָּרוּךְ אַתָּה יי, חַנּוּן הַמַּרְבֶּה
לִסְלֹחַ.

FORGIVE US, our Creator, when we sin; pardon us, our Sovereign, when we transgress; for You are eager to forgive.

We praise You, Eternal One, gracious and quick to forgive.

REDEMPTION   גאולה

רְאֵה בְעָנְיֵנוּ וְרִיבָה רִיבֵנוּ, וּגְאָלֵנוּ מְהֵרָה לְמַעַן שְׁמֶךָ,
כִּי גוֹאֵל חָזָק אָתָּה. בָּרוּךְ אַתָּה יי, גּוֹאֵל יִשְׂרָאֵל.

LOOK UPON OUR AFFLICTION and help us in our need; O mighty Redeemer, redeem us speedily for Your name's sake.

We praise You, Eternal One, Redeemer of Israel.

HEALTH   רפואה

רְפָאֵנוּ יי וְנֵרָפֵא, הוֹשִׁיעֵנוּ וְנִוָּשֵׁעָה, וְהַעֲלֵה רְפוּאָה
שְׁלֵמָה לְכָל־מַכּוֹתֵינוּ. בָּרוּךְ אַתָּה יי, רוֹפֵא הַחוֹלִים.

COMPASSIONATE SOURCE OF HEALING, heal us, and we shall be healed; save us, and we shall be saved; grant us a perfect healing for all our infirmities.

(A personal prayer for one who is ill may be added here.)

We praise You, Eternal One, Healer of the sick.

ABUNDANCE · ברכת השנים

בָּרֵךְ עָלֵינוּ, יי אֱלֹהֵינוּ, אֶת־הַשָּׁנָה הַזֹּאת וְאֶת־כָּל־מִינֵי
תְבוּאָתָהּ לְטוֹבָה. וְתֵן בְּרָכָה עַל־פְּנֵי הָאֲדָמָה
וְשַׂבְּעֵנוּ מִטּוּבֶךָ. בָּרוּךְ אַתָּה יי, מְבָרֵךְ הַשָּׁנִים.

BLESS THIS YEAR for us, Eternal God: may its produce bring us
well-being. Bestow Your blessing on the earth that all Your children may share its abundance in peace.

We praise You, Eternal One, for You bless earth's seasons from
year to year.

FREEDOM · חרות

תְּקַע בְּשׁוֹפָר גָּדוֹל לְחֵרוּתֵנוּ, וְשָׂא נֵס לִפְדּוֹת עֲשׁוּקֵינוּ,
וְקוֹל דְּרוֹר יִשָּׁמַע בְּאַרְבַּע כַּנְפוֹת הָאָרֶץ.
בָּרוּךְ אַתָּה יי, פּוֹדֶה עֲשׁוּקִים.

SOUND THE GREAT SHOFAR to proclaim freedom, raise high the
banner of liberation for the oppressed, and let the song of liberty
be heard in the four corners of the earth.

We praise You, Eternal One, Redeemer of the oppressed.

JUSTICE · משפט

עַל שׁוֹפְטֵי אֶרֶץ שְׁפוֹךְ רוּחֶךָ, וְהַדְרִיכֵם בְּמִשְׁפְּטֵי צִדְקֶךָ,
וּמְלוֹךְ עָלֵינוּ אַתָּה לְבַדֶּךָ, בְּחֶסֶד וּבְרַחֲמִים.
בָּרוּךְ אַתָּה יי, מֶלֶךְ אוֹהֵב צְדָקָה וּמִשְׁפָּט.

BESTOW YOUR SPIRIT upon the rulers of all lands; guide them,
that they may govern justly. Then shall love and compassion be
enthroned among us.

We praise You, Eternal One, the Sovereign God who loves
righteousness and justice.

ON EVIL   עַל הָרִשְׁעָה

וְלָרִשְׁעָה אַל־תְּהִי תִקְוָה, וְהַתּוֹעִים אֵלֶיךָ יָשׁוּבוּ, וּמַלְכוּת זָדוֹן מְהֵרָה תְשַׁבֵּר. תַּקֵּן מַלְכוּתְךָ בְּתוֹכֵנוּ, בְּקָרוֹב בְּיָמֵינוּ לְעוֹלָם וָעֶד. בָּרוּךְ אַתָּה יי, הַמַּשְׁבִּית רֶשַׁע מִן־הָאָרֶץ.

LET THE REIGN OF EVIL afflict us no more. May every errant heart find its way back to You. O help us to shatter the dominion of arrogance, to raise up a better world, where virtue will ennoble the life of Your children.

We praise You, Eternal One, whose will it is that evil vanish from the earth.

THE RIGHTEOUS   עַל הַצַּדִּיקִים

עַל־הַצַּדִּיקִים וְעַל־הַחֲסִידִים וְעַל גֵּרֵי הַצֶּדֶק וְעָלֵינוּ יֶהֱמוּ רַחֲמֶיךָ, יי אֱלֹהֵינוּ, וְתֵן שָׂכָר טוֹב לְכֹל הַבּוֹטְחִים בְּשִׁמְךָ בֶּאֱמֶת, וְשִׂים חֶלְקֵנוּ עִמָּהֶם לְעוֹלָם. בָּרוּךְ אַתָּה יי, מִשְׁעָן וּמִבְטָח לַצַּדִּיקִים.

FOR THE RIGHTEOUS AND FAITHFUL of all humankind, for all who join themselves to our people, for all who put their trust in You, and for all honest men and women, we ask Your favor, Eternal God. Grant that we may always be numbered among them.

We praise You, Eternal One, Staff and Support of the righteous.

JERUSALEM   בּוֹנֵה יְרוּשָׁלַיִם

שְׁכוֹן, יי אֱלֹהֵינוּ, בְּתוֹךְ יְרוּשָׁלַיִם עִירֶךָ, וִיהִי שָׁלוֹם בִּשְׁעָרֶיהָ, וְשַׁלְוָה בְּלֵב יוֹשְׁבֶיהָ, וְתוֹרָתְךָ מִצִּיּוֹן תֵּצֵא, וּדְבָרְךָ מִירוּשָׁלָיִם. בָּרוּךְ אַתָּה יי, בּוֹנֵה יְרוּשָׁלָיִם.

LET YOUR PRESENCE be manifest in Jerusalem, Your city. Establish peace in her gates and quietness in the hearts of all who dwell there. Let Your Torah go forth from Zion, Your word from Jerusalem.

We praise You, Eternal One, Builder of Jerusalem.

DELIVERANCE   ישועה

אֶת־צֶמַח צְדָקָה מְהֵרָה תַצְמִיחַ, וְקֶרֶן יְשׁוּעָה תָּרוּם
כִּנְאֻמֶךָ, כִּי לִישׁוּעָתְךָ קִוִּינוּ כָּל־הַיּוֹם.
בָּרוּךְ אַתָּה יי, מַצְמִיחַ קֶרֶן יְשׁוּעָה.

LET THE PLANT OF RIGHTEOUSNESS blossom and flourish, and let the light of deliverance shine forth according to Your word: we await Your deliverance all the day.

We praise You, Eternal One, who will cause the light of deliverance to dawn for all the world.

PRAYER   שומע תפלה

שְׁמַע קוֹלֵנוּ, יי אֱלֹהֵינוּ, חוּס וְרַחֵם עָלֵינוּ, וּתְקַבֵּל
בְּרַחֲמִים וּבְרָצוֹן אֶת־תְּפִלָּתֵנוּ, כִּי אֵל שׁוֹמֵעַ תְּפִלּוֹת
וְתַחֲנוּנִים אָתָּה. בָּרוּךְ אַתָּה יי, שׁוֹמֵעַ תְּפִלָּה.

HEAR OUR VOICE, ETERNAL GOD; have compassion upon us, and accept our prayer with favor and mercy, for You are a God who hears prayer and supplication.

We praise You, Eternal One, who hearkens to prayer.

❖ ❖

WORSHIP   עבודה

רְצֵה, יי אֱלֹהֵינוּ, בְּעַמְּךָ יִשְׂרָאֵל, וּתְפִלָּתָם בְּאַהֲבָה
תְקַבֵּל, וּתְהִי לְרָצוֹן תָּמִיד עֲבוֹדַת יִשְׂרָאֵל עַמֶּךָ.
אֵל קָרוֹב לְכָל־קֹרְאָיו, פְּנֵה אֶל עֲבָדֶיךָ וְחָנֵּנוּ;

18

שְׁפוֹךְ רוּחֲךָ עָלֵינוּ, וְתֶחֱזֶינָה עֵינֵינוּ בְּשׁוּבְךָ לְצִיּוֹן בְּרַחֲמִים.

בָּרוּךְ אַתָּה יי, הַמַּחֲזִיר שְׁכִינָתוֹ לְצִיּוֹן.

Be gracious, Eternal God, to Your people Israel, and receive our prayers with love. O may our worship always be acceptable to You.

Fill us with the knowledge that You are near to all who seek You in truth. Let our eyes behold Your presence in our midst and in the midst of our people in Zion. We praise You, Eternal One, whose presence gives life to Zion and all Israel.

ON ROSH CHODESH AND CHOL HAMO-EID :

אֱלֹהֵינוּ וֵאלֹהֵי אֲבוֹתֵינוּ וְאִמּוֹתֵינוּ, יַעֲלֶה וְיָבֹא וְיִזָּכֵר
זִכְרוֹנֵנוּ וְזִכְרוֹן כָּל־עַמְּךָ בֵּית יִשְׂרָאֵל לְפָנֶיךָ לְטוֹבָה
לְחֵן לְחֶסֶד וּלְרַחֲמִים, לְחַיִּים וּלְשָׁלוֹם בְּיוֹם

Our God, God of our fathers and our mothers, be mindful of Your people Israel on this

• first day of the new month,   רֹאשׁ הַחֹדֶשׁ הַזֶּה.•

• day of Pesach,   חַג הַמַּצּוֹת הַזֶּה.•

• day of Sukkot,   חַג הַסֻּכּוֹת הַזֶּה.•

זָכְרֵנוּ, יי אֱלֹהֵינוּ, בּוֹ לְטוֹבָה. אָמֵן.

וּפָקְדֵנוּ בוֹ לִבְרָכָה. אָמֵן.

וְהוֹשִׁיעֵנוּ בוֹ לְחַיִּים. אָמֵן.

and renew in us love and compassion, goodness, life, and peace.
This day remember us for well-being. *Amen.*
This day bless us with Your nearness. *Amen.*
This day help us to lead a full life. *Amen.*

THANKSGIVING   הודאה

מוֹדִים אֲנַחְנוּ לָךְ, שָׁאַתָּה הוּא יי אֱלֹהֵינוּ וֵאלֹהֵי
אֲבוֹתֵינוּ וְאִמּוֹתֵינוּ לְעוֹלָם וָעֶד. צוּר חַיֵּינוּ, מָגֵן יִשְׁעֵנוּ,

19

אַתָּה הוּא לְדוֹר וָדוֹר. נוֹדֶה לְךָ וּנְסַפֵּר תְּהִלָּתֶךָ, עַל־
חַיֵּינוּ הַמְּסוּרִים בְּיָדֶךָ, וְעַל־נִשְׁמוֹתֵינוּ הַפְּקוּדוֹת לָךְ,
וְעַל־נִסֶּיךָ שֶׁבְּכָל־יוֹם עִמָּנוּ, וְעַל־נִפְלְאוֹתֶיךָ וְטוֹבוֹתֶיךָ
שֶׁבְּכָל־עֵת, עֶרֶב וָבֹקֶר וְצָהֳרָיִם. הַטּוֹב: כִּי לֹא־כָלוּ
רַחֲמֶיךָ, וְהַמְרַחֵם: כִּי־לֹא תַמּוּ חֲסָדֶיךָ, מֵעוֹלָם קִוִּינוּ
לָךְ. וְעַל כֻּלָּם יִתְבָּרַךְ וְיִתְרוֹמַם שִׁמְךָ, מַלְכֵּנוּ, תָּמִיד
לְעוֹלָם וָעֶד.

BETWEEN ROSH HASHANAH AND YOM KIPPUR ADD:

וּכְתוֹב לְחַיִּים טוֹבִים כָּל־בְּנֵי בְרִיתֶךָ.

וְכֹל הַחַיִּים יוֹדְוּךָ סֶּלָה, וִיהַלְלוּ אֶת שִׁמְךָ בֶּאֱמֶת,
הָאֵל יְשׁוּעָתֵנוּ וְעֶזְרָתֵנוּ סֶלָה.
בָּרוּךְ אַתָּה יי, הַטּוֹב שִׁמְךָ וּלְךָ נָאֶה לְהוֹדוֹת.

*We gratefully acknowledge that You are our God and the
God of our people, the God of all the generations. You are
the Rock of our life, the Power that shields us in every age.
We thank You and sing Your praises: for our lives, which
are in Your hand; for our souls, which are in Your keeping;
for the signs of Your presence we encounter every day; and
for Your wondrous gifts at all times, morning, noon, and
night. You are Goodness: Your mercies never end; You are
Compassion: Your love will never fail. You have always
been our hope.*

For all these things, O Sovereign God, let Your name be for ever
exalted and blessed.

BETWEEN ROSH HASHANAH AND YOM KIPPUR ADD:

May all who are loyal to Your covenant
be inscribed for a good life.

O God our Redeemer and Helper, let all who live affirm You and praise Your name in truth. Eternal God, whose nature is Goodness, we give You thanks and praise.

❖ ❖

ON CHANUKAH ADD:

עַל הַנִּסִּים וְעַל הַפֻּרְקָן, וְעַל הַגְּבוּרוֹת וְעַל הַתְּשׁוּעוֹת, וְעַל
הַמִּלְחָמוֹת, שֶׁעָשִׂיתָ לַאֲבוֹתֵינוּ וּלְאִמּוֹתֵינוּ בַּיָּמִים הָהֵם בַּזְּמַן הַזֶּה.
בִּימֵי מַתִּתְיָהוּ בֶּן־יוֹחָנָן כֹּהֵן גָּדוֹל, חַשְׁמוֹנַאי וּבָנָיו, כְּשֶׁעָמְדָה
מַלְכוּת יָוָן הָרְשָׁעָה עַל עַמְּךָ יִשְׂרָאֵל, לְהַשְׁכִּיחָם תּוֹרָתֶךָ
וּלְהַעֲבִירָם מֵחֻקֵּי רְצוֹנֶךָ. וְאַתָּה בְּרַחֲמֶיךָ הָרַבִּים עָמַדְתָּ לָהֶם
בְּעֵת צָרָתָם, רַבְתָּ אֶת־רִיבָם, דַּנְתָּ אֶת־דִּינָם, נָקַמְתָּ אֶת־נִקְמָתָם,
מָסַרְתָּ גִבּוֹרִים בְּיַד חַלָּשִׁים, וְרַבִּים בְּיַד מְעַטִּים, וּטְמֵאִים בְּיַד
טְהוֹרִים, וּרְשָׁעִים בְּיַד צַדִּיקִים, וְזֵדִים בְּיַד עוֹסְקֵי תוֹרָתֶךָ. וּלְךָ
עָשִׂיתָ שֵׁם גָּדוֹל וְקָדוֹשׁ בְּעוֹלָמֶךָ, וּלְעַמְּךָ יִשְׂרָאֵל עָשִׂיתָ תְּשׁוּעָה
גְדוֹלָה וּפֻרְקָן כְּהַיּוֹם הַזֶּה. וְאַחַר כֵּן בָּאוּ בָנֶיךָ לִדְבִיר בֵּיתֶךָ, וּפִנּוּ
אֶת־הֵיכָלֶךָ, וְטִהֲרוּ אֶת־מִקְדָּשֶׁךָ, וְהִדְלִיקוּ נֵרוֹת בְּחַצְרוֹת קָדְשֶׁךָ,
וְקָבְעוּ שְׁמוֹנַת יְמֵי חֲנֻכָּה אֵלּוּ, לְהוֹדוֹת וּלְהַלֵּל לְשִׁמְךָ הַגָּדוֹל.

In days of old at this season You saved our people by wonders and mighty deeds. In the days of Mattathias the Hasmonean, the Hellenic Empire sought to destroy our people Israel, by making them forget their Torah, and by forcing them to abandon their ancient way of life.

Through the power of Your spirit the weak defeated the strong, the few prevailed over the many, and the righteous were victorious. Then Your children returned to Your house to purify the sanctuary and to kindle its lights. And they dedicated these days to give thanks and praise to Your majestic glory.

ON PURIM ADD:

עַל הַנִּסִּים וְעַל הַפֻּרְקָן, וְעַל הַגְּבוּרוֹת וְעַל הַתְּשׁוּעוֹת, וְעַל
הַמִּלְחָמוֹת, שֶׁעָשִׂיתָ לַאֲבוֹתֵינוּ וּלְאִמּוֹתֵינוּ בַּיָּמִים הָהֵם בַּזְּמַן הַזֶּה.
בִּימֵי מָרְדְּכַי וְאֶסְתֵּר בְּשׁוּשַׁן הַבִּירָה, כְּשֶׁעָמַד עֲלֵיהֶם הָמָן הָרָשָׁע,
בִּקֵּשׁ לְהַשְׁמִיד לַהֲרֹג וּלְאַבֵּד אֶת־כָּל־הַיְּהוּדִים, מִנַּעַר וְעַד־זָקֵן,

טַף וְנָשִׁים, בְּיוֹם אֶחָד, בִּשְׁלֹשָׁה עָשָׂר לְחֹדֶשׁ שְׁנֵים־עָשָׂר, הוּא־
חֹדֶשׁ אֲדָר, וּשְׁלָלָם לָבוֹז. וְאַתָּה בְּרַחֲמֶיךָ הָרַבִּים הֵפַרְתָּ
אֶת־עֲצָתוֹ וְקִלְקַלְתָּ אֶת־מַחֲשַׁבְתּוֹ.

In days of old at this season You saved our people by wonders and mighty deeds. In the days of Mordechai and Esther, the wicked Haman arose in Persia, plotting the destruction of all the Jews. He planned to destroy them in a single day, the thirteenth of Adar, and to plunder their possessions.

But through Your great mercy, his plan was thwarted, his scheme frustrated. We therefore thank and bless You, the great and gracious God!

❖ ❖

PEACE   ברכת שלום

שָׁלוֹם רָב עַל־יִשְׂרָאֵל עַמְּךָ תָּשִׂים לְעוֹלָם,
כִּי אַתָּה הוּא מֶלֶךְ אָדוֹן לְכָל הַשָּׁלוֹם. וְטוֹב בְּעֵינֶיךָ
לְבָרֵךְ אֶת־עַמְּךָ יִשְׂרָאֵל בְּכָל־עֵת וּבְכָל־שָׁעָה בִּשְׁלוֹמֶךָ.
*בָּרוּךְ אַתָּה יי, הַמְבָרֵךְ אֶת־עַמּוֹ יִשְׂרָאֵל בַּשָּׁלוֹם.

*BETWEEN ROSH HASHANAH AND YOM KIPPUR CONCLUDE:

בְּסֵפֶר חַיִּים וּבְרָכָה נִכָּתֵב לְחַיִּים טוֹבִים וּלְשָׁלוֹם.
בָּרוּךְ אַתָּה יי, עוֹשֵׂה הַשָּׁלוֹם.

O Sovereign Source of peace, let Israel Your people know enduring peace, for it is good in Your sight to bless Israel continually with Your peace.

* *We praise You, Eternal One: You bless Israel with peace.*

*BETWEEN ROSH HASHANAH AND YOM KIPPUR CONCLUDE:

Inscribe us in the Book of life, blessing, and peace.
We praise You, Eternal One, the Source of peace.

SILENT PRAYER

אֱלֹהַי, נְצֹר לְשׁוֹנִי מֵרָע, וּשְׂפָתַי מִדַּבֵּר מִרְמָה. וְלִמְקַלְלַי
נַפְשִׁי תִדּוֹם וְנַפְשִׁי כֶּעָפָר לַכֹּל תִּהְיֶה. פְּתַח לִבִּי בְּתוֹרָתֶךָ,
וּבְמִצְוֹתֶיךָ תִּרְדּוֹף נַפְשִׁי. וְכָל־הַחוֹשְׁבִים עָלַי רָעָה, מְהֵרָה
הָפֵר עֲצָתָם וְקַלְקֵל מַחֲשַׁבְתָּם. עֲשֵׂה לְמַעַן שְׁמֶךָ, עֲשֵׂה
לְמַעַן יְמִינֶךָ, עֲשֵׂה לְמַעַן קְדֻשָּׁתֶךָ, עֲשֵׂה לְמַעַן תּוֹרָתֶךָ;
לְמַעַן יֵחָלְצוּן יְדִידֶיךָ, הוֹשִׁיעָה יְמִינְךָ וַעֲנֵנִי.

O God, keep my tongue from evil and my lips from deceit. Help
me to be silent in the face of derision, humble in the presence of
all. Open my heart to Your Torah, and I will hasten to do Your
Mitzvot. Save me with Your power; in time of trouble be my
answer, that those who love You may rejoice.

❖ ❖

יִהְיוּ לְרָצוֹן אִמְרֵי־פִי וְהֶגְיוֹן לִבִּי לְפָנֶיךָ, יהוה, צוּרִי וְגֹאֲלִי.

May the words of my mouth, and the meditations of my heart,
be acceptable to You, O God, my Rock and my Redeemer.

❖

עֹשֶׂה שָׁלוֹם בִּמְרוֹמָיו, הוּא יַעֲשֶׂה שָׁלוֹם עָלֵינוּ וְעַל־כָּל־
יִשְׂרָאֵל, וְאִמְרוּ אָמֵן.

O-seh sha-lom bim-ro-mav, hu ya-a-seh sha-lom a-lei-nu v'al kol
Yis-ra-eil, v'im-ru: A-mein.

May the One who causes peace to reign in the high heavens let
peace descend on us, on all Israel, and all the world.

Torah Service begins on page 68

Service at a House of Mourning begins on page 88

Aleinu is on page 74 or 77

Evening or Morning Service I

וְעַתָּה יִשְׂרָאֵל: מָה יהוה אֱלֹהֶיךָ שֹׁאֵל מֵעִמָּךְ?
כִּי אִם־לְיִרְאָה אֶת־יהוה אֱלֹהֶיךָ, לָלֶכֶת בְּכָל־דְּרָכָיו
וּלְאַהֲבָה אֹתוֹ, וְלַעֲבֹד אֶת־יהוה אֱלֹהֶיךָ בְּכָל־לְבָבְךָ
וּבְכָל־נַפְשֶׁךָ.

And now, O Israel, what is it that the Eternal One, your God,
asks of you?

"Show reverence for Me, Walk in My ways,
love and serve Me with all your heart and soul."

וְעַתָּה אִם־שָׁמוֹעַ תִּשְׁמְעוּ בְּקֹלִי וּשְׁמַרְתֶּם אֶת־בְּרִיתִי,
וִאַתֶּם תִּהְיוּ־לִי מַמְלֶכֶת כֹּהֲנִים, וְגוֹי קָדוֹשׁ.
לִפְקֹחַ עֵינַיִם עִוְרוֹת, לְהוֹצִיא מִמַּסְגֵּר אַסִּיר, מִבֵּית כֶּלֶא
יֹשְׁבֵי חֹשֶׁךְ.

Now therefore if you will truly keep My covenant,
you shall be to Me a consecrated family, a holy people:

To open blind eyes, to bring out of prison the captive,
and from their dungeons those who sit in darkness.

All rise

The Sh'ma and Its Blessings שמע וברכותיה

בָּרְכוּ אֶת־יי הַמְבֹרָךְ!

Praise the One to whom our praise is due!

בָּרוּךְ יי הַמְבֹרָךְ לְעוֹלָם וָעֶד!

Ba-ruch Adonai ha-m'vo-rach l'o-lam va-ed!

Praised be the One to whom our praise is due, now and for ever!

24

CREATION

EVENING

בָּרוּךְ אַתָּה יי, אֱלֹהֵינוּ מֶלֶךְ
הָעוֹלָם, אֲשֶׁר בִּדְבָרוֹ
מַעֲרִיב עֲרָבִים, בְּחָכְמָה
פּוֹתֵחַ שְׁעָרִים, וּבִתְבוּנָה
מְשַׁנֶּה עִתִּים, וּמַחֲלִיף אֶת־
הַזְּמַנִּים, וּמְסַדֵּר אֶת־
הַכּוֹכָבִים בְּמִשְׁמְרוֹתֵיהֶם
בָּרָקִיעַ כִּרְצוֹנוֹ. בּוֹרֵא יוֹם
וָלָיְלָה, גּוֹלֵל אוֹר מִפְּנֵי
חֹשֶׁךְ וְחֹשֶׁךְ מִפְּנֵי אוֹר,
וּמַעֲבִיר יוֹם וּמֵבִיא לָיְלָה,
וּמַבְדִּיל בֵּין יוֹם וּבֵין לָיְלָה,
יי צְבָאוֹת שְׁמוֹ. אֵל חַי
וְקַיָּם, תָּמִיד יִמְלוֹךְ עָלֵינוּ
לְעוֹלָם וָעֶד! בָּרוּךְ אַתָּה יי,
הַמַּעֲרִיב עֲרָבִים.

MORNING

בָּרוּךְ אַתָּה יי, אֱלֹהֵינוּ מֶלֶךְ
הָעוֹלָם, יוֹצֵר אוֹר וּבוֹרֵא
חֹשֶׁךְ, עֹשֶׂה שָׁלוֹם וּבוֹרֵא
אֶת־הַכֹּל. הַמֵּאִיר לָאָרֶץ
וְלַדָּרִים עָלֶיהָ בְּרַחֲמִים,
וּבְטוּבוֹ מְחַדֵּשׁ בְּכָל־יוֹם
תָּמִיד מַעֲשֵׂה בְרֵאשִׁית.
מָה רַבּוּ מַעֲשֶׂיךָ יי! כֻּלָּם
בְּחָכְמָה עָשִׂיתָ, מָלְאָה
הָאָרֶץ קִנְיָנֶךָ. תִּתְבָּרַךְ, יי
אֱלֹהֵינוּ, עַל־שֶׁבַח מַעֲשֵׂה
יָדֶיךָ, וְעַל־מְאוֹרֵי־אוֹר
שֶׁעָשִׂיתָ: יְפָאֲרוּךָ. סֶלָה.
בָּרוּךְ אַתָּה יי, יוֹצֵר
הַמְּאוֹרוֹת.

° Eternal God, Your majesty is proclaimed by the marvels of earth and sky. Sun, moon, and stars testify to Your power and wisdom. Day follows day in endless succession, and the years vanish, but Your sovereignty endures. Though all things pass, let not Your glory depart from us. Help us to become co-workers with You, and endow our fleeting days with abiding worth.

REVELATION

EVENING   **MORNING**

אַהֲבָה רַבָּה אֲהַבְתָּנוּ, יי
אֱלֹהֵינוּ, חֶמְלָה גְדוֹלָה וִיתֵרָה
חָמַלְתָּ עָלֵינוּ. אָבִינוּ מַלְכֵּנוּ,
בַּעֲבוּר אֲבוֹתֵינוּ וְאִמּוֹתֵינוּ
שֶׁבָּטְחוּ בְךָ וַתְּלַמְּדֵם חֻקֵּי
חַיִּים, כֵּן תְּחָנֵּנוּ וּתְלַמְּדֵנוּ.
אָבִינוּ, הָאָב הָרַחֲמָן,
הַמְרַחֵם, רַחֵם עָלֵינוּ וְתֵן
בְּלִבֵּנוּ לְהָבִין וּלְהַשְׂכִּיל,
לִשְׁמֹעַ לִלְמֹד וּלְלַמֵּד, לִשְׁמֹר
וְלַעֲשׂוֹת וּלְקַיֵּם אֶת־כָּל־דִּבְרֵי
תַלְמוּד תּוֹרָתֶךָ בְּאַהֲבָה.

וְהָאֵר עֵינֵינוּ בְּתוֹרָתֶךָ, וְדַבֵּק

אַהֲבַת עוֹלָם בֵּית יִשְׂרָאֵל
עַמְּךָ אָהַבְתָּ. תּוֹרָה וּמִצְוֹת,
חֻקִּים וּמִשְׁפָּטִים אוֹתָנוּ
לִמַּדְתָּ. עַל־כֵּן, יי אֱלֹהֵינוּ,
בְּשָׁכְבֵּנוּ וּבְקוּמֵנוּ נָשִׂיחַ
בְּחֻקֶּיךָ, וְנִשְׂמַח בְּדִבְרֵי
תוֹרָתְךָ וּבְמִצְוֹתֶיךָ לְעוֹלָם
וָעֶד. כִּי הֵם חַיֵּינוּ וְאֹרֶךְ
יָמֵינוּ, וּבָהֶם נֶהְגֶּה יוֹמָם
וָלָיְלָה. וְאַהֲבָתְךָ אַל־תָּסוּר
מִמֶּנּוּ לְעוֹלָמִים! בָּרוּךְ אַתָּה
יי, אוֹהֵב עַמּוֹ יִשְׂרָאֵל.

לִבֵּנוּ בְּמִצְוֹתֶיךָ, וְיַחֵד לְבָבֵנוּ לְאַהֲבָה וּלְיִרְאָה אֶת־שְׁמֶךָ.
וְלֹא־נֵבוֹשׁ לְעוֹלָם וָעֶד, כִּי בְשֵׁם קָדְשְׁךָ הַגָּדוֹל וְהַנּוֹרָא
בָּטָחְנוּ. נָגִילָה וְנִשְׂמְחָה בִּישׁוּעָתֶךָ, כִּי אֵל פּוֹעֵל יְשׁוּעוֹת
אָתָּה, וּבָנוּ בָחַרְתָּ וְקֵרַבְתָּנוּ לְשִׁמְךָ הַגָּדוֹל סֶלָה בֶּאֱמֶת,
לְהוֹדוֹת לְךָ וּלְיַחֶדְךָ בְּאַהֲבָה. בָּרוּךְ אַתָּה יי, הַבּוֹחֵר בְּעַמּוֹ
יִשְׂרָאֵל בְּאַהֲבָה.

° *You are our God, the Source of life and its blessings.*
Wherever we turn our gaze, we behold signs of Your
goodness and love. The whole universe proclaims Your
glory. Your loving spirit hovers over all Your works,
guiding and sustaining them. The harmony and grandeur
of nature speak to us of You; the beauty and truth of Torah
reveal Your will to us. You are the One and Eternal God of
time and space!

שְׁמַע יִשְׂרָאֵל: יהוה אֱלֹהֵינוּ, יהוה אֶחָד!

Sh'ma Yis-ra-eil: Adonai Eh-lo-hei-nu, Adonai Eh-chad!

Hear, O Israel: the Eternal One is our God,
the Eternal God alone!

בָּרוּךְ שֵׁם כְּבוֹד מַלְכוּתוֹ לְעוֹלָם וָעֶד!

Ba-ruch sheim k'vod mal-chu-toh l'o-lam va-ed!

Blessed is God's glorious majesty for ever and ever!

All are seated

וְאָהַבְתָּ אֵת יהוה אֱלֹהֶיךָ בְּכָל־לְבָבְךָ וּבְכָל־נַפְשְׁךָ
וּבְכָל־מְאֹדֶךָ: וְהָיוּ הַדְּבָרִים הָאֵלֶּה אֲשֶׁר אָנֹכִי מְצַוְּךָ
הַיּוֹם עַל־לְבָבֶךָ: וְשִׁנַּנְתָּם לְבָנֶיךָ וְדִבַּרְתָּ בָּם בְּשִׁבְתְּךָ
בְּבֵיתֶךָ וּבְלֶכְתְּךָ בַדֶּרֶךְ וּבְשָׁכְבְּךָ וּבְקוּמֶךָ: וּקְשַׁרְתָּם
לְאוֹת עַל־יָדֶךָ וְהָיוּ לְטֹטָפֹת בֵּין עֵינֶיךָ: וּכְתַבְתָּם
עַל־מְזֻזֹת בֵּיתֶךָ וּבִשְׁעָרֶיךָ:

V'a-hav-ta et Adonai Eh-lo-heh-cha b'chol l'va-v'cha u-v'chol naf-
sh'cha u-v'chol m'o-deh-cha. V'ha-yu ha-d'va-rim ha-ei-leh a-sher
a-no-chi m'tza-v'cha ha-yom al l'va-veh-cha. V'shi-nan-tam l'va-neh-
cha v'di-bar-ta bam b'shiv-t'cha b'vei-teh-cha u-v'lech-t'cha va-deh-
rech u-v'shoch-b'cha u-v'ku-meh-cha. U-k'shar-tam l'oht al ya-deh-
cha v'ha-yu l'toh-ta-foht bein ei-neh-cha; u-ch'tav-tam al m'zu-zoht
bei-teh-cha u-vi-sh'a-reh-cha.

*You shall love the Eternal One, your God, with all your
heart, with all your mind, with all your being. Set these
words, which I command you this day, upon your heart.
Teach them faithfully to your children; speak of them in
your home and on your way, when you lie down and when
you rise up. Bind them as a sign upon your hand; let them
be a symbol before your eyes; inscribe them on the door-
posts of your house, and on your gates.*

לְמַעַן תִּזְכְּרוּ וַעֲשִׂיתֶם אֶת־כָּל־מִצְוֹתָי וִהְיִיתֶם קְדשִׁים
לֵאלֹהֵיכֶם: אֲנִי יהוה אֱלֹהֵיכֶם אֲשֶׁר הוֹצֵאתִי אֶתְכֶם
מֵאֶרֶץ מִצְרַיִם לִהְיוֹת לָכֶם לֵאלֹהִים אֲנִי יהוה אֱלֹהֵיכֶם:

L'ma-an tiz-k'ru va-a-si-tem et kol mitz-vo-tai, vi-h'yi-tem k'doh-shim
lei-lo-hei-chem. A-ni Adonai Eh-lo-hei-chem a-sher ho-tzei-ti et-chem
mei-eh-retz mitz-ra-yim li-h'yoht la-chem lei-lo-him. A-ni Adonai
Eh-lo-hei-chem.

*Be mindful of all My Mitzvot, and do them: so shall you
consecrate yourselves to your God. I am your Eternal God
who led you out of Egypt to be your God; I am your Eternal
God.*

REDEMPTION   גאולה

אֲנִי, יהוה, קְרָאתִיךָ בְצֶדֶק וְאַחְזֵק בְּיָדֶךָ,
וְאֶצָּרְךָ; וְאֶתֶּנְךָ לִבְרִית עָם, לְאוֹר גּוֹיִם.

° I, the Eternal One, have called you to righteousness, and taken
you by the hand, and kept you; I have made you a covenant people, a light to the nations.

*We are Israel: witness to the covenant between
God and God's children.*

כִּי זֹאת הַבְּרִית אֲשֶׁר אֶכְרֹת אֶת־בֵּית יִשְׂרָאֵל:
נָתַתִּי אֶת־תּוֹרָתִי בְּקִרְבָּם, וְעַל־לִבָּם אֶכְתֶּבֶנָּה.
וְהָיִיתִי לָהֶם לֵאלֹהִים, וְהֵמָּה יִהְיוּ־לִי לְעָם.

"This is the covenant I make with Israel: I will place My Torah
in your midst, and write it upon your hearts. I will be your God,
and you will be My people."

*We are Israel: our Torah forbids the worship of race or
nation, possessions or power.*

הַמִּתְפַּלְלִים אֶל־אֵל לֹא יוֹשִׁיעַ, שִׁמְעוּ דְּבַר־יהוה:
"הֲלוֹא אֲנִי יהוה, וְאֵין־עוֹד אֱלֹהִים מִבַּלְעָדָי!"

"You who worship gods that cannot save you, hear the words of the Eternal One: 'I am God, there is none else!'"

We are Israel: our prophets proclaimed
an exalted vision for the world.

שִׂנְאוּ־רָע וְאֶהֱבוּ טוֹב.
וְיִגַּל כַּמַּיִם מִשְׁפָּט וּצְדָקָה כְּנַחַל אֵיתָן.

"Hate evil, and love what is good; let justice well up as waters and righteousness as a mighty stream."

We are Israel, schooled in the suffering of the oppressed.

לֹא־תַעֲשֹׁק אֶת־רֵעֲךָ וְלֹא תִגְזֹל. לֹא תַעֲמֹד עַל־דַּם רֵעֶךָ.

"You shall not oppress your neighbors nor rob them.
You shall not stand idle while your neighbor bleeds"

We are Israel, taught to beat swords into plowshares,
commanded to pursue peace.

לֹא־יִשָּׁמַע עוֹד חָמָס בְּאַרְצֵךְ, שֹׁד וָשֶׁבֶר בִּגְבוּלָיִךְ.
וְכָל־בָּנַיִךְ לִמּוּדֵי יהוה, וְרַב שְׁלוֹם בָּנָיִךְ.

"Violence shall no longer be heard in your land, desolation and destruction within your borders. All your children will be taught of your God, and great shall be the peace of your children."

We are Israel, O God, when we are witnesses to Your love
and messengers of Your truth.

אַתֶּם עֵדַי, נְאֻם־יהוה, וְעַבְדִּי אֲשֶׁר בָּחָרְתִּי;
לְמַעַן תֵּדְעוּ וְתַאֲמִינוּ לִי.

"You are My witnesses," says the Eternal One, "and My servant whom I have chosen; know Me, therefore, and put your trust in Me."

We are Israel, O God,
when we proclaim You God our Redeemer,
as did our ancestors on the shores of the Sea:

29

מִי־כָמְכָה בָּאֵלִם, יהוה? מִי כָּמְכָה, נֶאְדָּר בַּקֹּדֶשׁ,
נוֹרָא תְהִלֹת, עֹשֵׂה פֶלֶא?

Mi cha-mo-cha ba-ei-lim, Adonai? Mi ka-mo-cha, neh-dar ba-ko-desh, no-ra t'hi-loht, o-sei feh-leh?

EVENING

מַלְכוּתְךָ רָאוּ בָנֶיךָ, בּוֹקֵעַ יָם
לִפְנֵי מֹשֶׁה; זֶה אֵלִי! עָנוּ
וְאָמְרוּ: יהוה יִמְלֹךְ לְעֹלָם
וָעֶד!

וְנֶאֱמַר: כִּי פָדָה יי אֶת־
יַעֲקֹב, וּגְאָלוֹ מִיַּד חָזָק מִמֶּנּוּ.
בָּרוּךְ אַתָּה יי, גָּאַל יִשְׂרָאֵל.

MORNING

שִׁירָה חֲדָשָׁה שִׁבְּחוּ גְאוּלִים
לְשִׁמְךָ עַל־שְׂפַת הַיָּם; יַחַד
כֻּלָּם הוֹדוּ וְהִמְלִיכוּ וְאָמְרוּ:
"יי יִמְלֹךְ לְעוֹלָם וָעֶד!"

צוּר יִשְׂרָאֵל, קוּמָה בְּעֶזְרַת
יִשְׂרָאֵל, וּפְדֵה כִנְאֻמֶךָ יְהוּדָה
וְיִשְׂרָאֵל. גֹּאֲלֵנוּ יי צְבָאוֹת
שְׁמוֹ, קְדוֹשׁ יִשְׂרָאֵל.
בָּרוּךְ אַתָּה, יי, גָּאַל יִשְׂרָאֵל.

Who is like You, Eternal One, among the gods that are worshipped? Who is like You, majestic in holiness, awesome in splendor, doing wonders?

When Your children perceived Your power they exclaimed: "This is my God!" "The Eternal One will reign for ever and ever!"

30

All rise

תפלה T'filah

אֲדֹנָי, שְׂפָתַי תִּפְתָּח וּפִי יַגִּיד תְּהִלָּתֶךָ.

Eternal God, open my lips, that my mouth may declare Your glory.

GOD OF ALL GENERATIONS   אבות ואמהות

בָּרוּךְ אַתָּה יי, אֱלֹהֵינוּ וֵאלֹהֵי אֲבוֹתֵינוּ וְאִמּוֹתֵינוּ:
אֱלֹהֵי אַבְרָהָם, אֱלֹהֵי יִצְחָק, וֵאלֹהֵי יַעֲקֹב.
אֱלֹהֵי שָׂרָה, אֱלֹהֵי רִבְקָה, אֱלֹהֵי לֵאָה, וֵאלֹהֵי רָחֵל.
הָאֵל הַגָּדוֹל הַגִּבּוֹר וְהַנּוֹרָא, אֵל עֶלְיוֹן, גּוֹמֵל חֲסָדִים
טוֹבִים וְקוֹנֵה הַכֹּל, וְזוֹכֵר חַסְדֵי אָבוֹת וְאִמָּהוֹת,
וּמֵבִיא גְאֻלָּה לִבְנֵי בְנֵיהֶם, לְמַעַן שְׁמוֹ בְּאַהֲבָה.

BETWEEN ROSH HASHANAH AND YOM KIPPUR ADD:

זָכְרֵנוּ לְחַיִּים, מֶלֶךְ חָפֵץ בַּחַיִּים,
וְכָתְבֵנוּ בְּסֵפֶר הַחַיִּים, לְמַעַנְךָ אֱלֹהִים חַיִּים.

מֶלֶךְ עוֹזֵר וּמוֹשִׁיעַ וּמָגֵן.
בָּרוּךְ אַתָּה יי, מָגֵן אַבְרָהָם וְעֶזְרַת שָׂרָה.

Ba-ruch a-ta Adonai, Eh-lo-hei-nu vei-lo-hei a-vo-tei-nu v'i-mo-tei-nu:
Eh-lo-hei Av-ra-ham, Eh-lo-hei Yitz-chak, vei-lo-hei Ya-a-kov. Eh-lo-
hei Sa-rah, Eh-lo-hei Riv-kah, Eh-lo-hei Lei-ah, vei-lo-hei Ra-cheil.
Ha-eil ha-ga-dol ha-gi-bor v'ha-no-ra, Eil el-yon. Go-meil cha-sa-dim
toh-vim, v'ko-nei ha-kol, v'zo-cheir chas-dei a-voht v'i-ma-hoht,
u-mei-vi g'u-la li-v'nei v'nei-hem, l'ma-an sh'mo, b'a-ha-va.

BETWEEN ROSH HASHANAH AND YOM KIPPUR ADD:

Zoch'rei-nu l'cha-yim, meh-lech cha-feitz ba-cha-yim,
v'cho-t'vei-nu b'sei-fer ha-cha-yim, l'ma-an-cha Eh-lo-him cha-yim.

Meh-lech o-zeir u-mo-shi-a u-ma-gein.
Ba-ruch a-ta Adonai, ma-gein Av-ra-ham v'ez-rat Sa-rah.

Praised be the Eternal One, our God, God of our fathers and our mothers, God of Abraham, God of Isaac, and God of Jacob, God of Sarah, God of Rebekah, God of Leah and God of Rachel, great, mighty, and exalted.

You bestow love and kindness on all Your children. You remember the devotion of ages past. In Your love, You bring redemption to their descendants for the sake of Your name.

BETWEEN ROSH HASHANAH AND YOM KIPPUR ADD:

Remember us unto life, Sovereign who delights in life, and inscribe us in the Book of Life, that Your will may prevail, O God of life.

You are our Ruler and Helper, our Savior and Protector. We praise You, Eternal One, Shield of Abraham, Protector of Sarah.

GOD'S POWER   גבורות

אַתָּה גִבּוֹר לְעוֹלָם, אֲדֹנָי, מְחַיֵּה הַכֹּל אַתָּה, רַב לְהוֹשִׁיעַ.
מְכַלְכֵּל חַיִּים בְּחֶסֶד, מְחַיֵּה הַכֹּל בְּרַחֲמִים רַבִּים. סוֹמֵךְ
נוֹפְלִים, וְרוֹפֵא חוֹלִים, וּמַתִּיר אֲסוּרִים, וּמְקַיֵּם אֱמוּנָתוֹ
לִישֵׁנֵי עָפָר. מִי כָמְוֹךָ בַּעַל גְּבוּרוֹת, וּמִי דּוֹמֶה לָּךְ, מֶלֶךְ
מֵמִית וּמְחַיֵּה וּמַצְמִיחַ יְשׁוּעָה?

BETWEEN ROSH HASHANAH AND YOM KIPPUR ADD:

מִי כָמְוֹךָ, אֵל הָרַחֲמִים, זוֹכֵר יְצוּרָיו לְחַיִּים בְּרַחֲמִים?

וְנֶאֱמָן אַתָּה לְהַחֲיוֹת הַכֹּל. בָּרוּךְ אַתָּה יי, מְחַיֵּה הַכֹּל.

A-ta gi-bor l'o-lam, Adonai, m'cha-yei ha-kol a-ta, rav l'ho-shi-a. M'chal-keil cha-yim b'cheh-sed, m'cha-yei ha-kol b'ra-cha-mim ra-bim. So-meich no-f'lim, v'ro-fei cho-lim, u-ma-tir a-su-rim, u-m'ka-yeim eh-mu-na-toh li-shei-nei a-far. Mi cha-mo-cha ba-al g'vu-roht, u-mi doh-meh lach, meh-lech mei-mit u-m'cha-yeh u-matz-mi-ach y'shu-a?

BETWEEN ROSH HASHANAH AND YOM KIPPUR ADD:

Mi cha-mo-cha, Eil ha-ra-cha-mim, zo-cheir y'tzu-rav l'cha-yim b'ra-cha-mim?

V'neh-eh-man a-ta l'ha-cha-yoht ha-kol. Ba-ruch a-ta Adonai, m'cha-yei ha-kol.

Eternal is Your might, O God, and great is Your saving power. In love You sustain the living; in Your great mercy, You sustain us all. You uphold the falling and heal the sick; free the captive and keep faith with Your children in death as in life.

Who is like You, almighty God, Author of life and death, Source of salvation?

BETWEEN ROSH HASHANAH AND YOM KIPPUR ADD:

Who is like You, Source of mercy?
In compassion You sustain the life of Your children.

We praise You, Eternal One, the Source of life.

FOR AN EVENING SERVICE

THE HOLINESS OF GOD   קדושת השם

אַתָּה קָדוֹשׁ וְשִׁמְךָ קָדוֹשׁ, וּקְדוֹשִׁים בְּכָל־יוֹם יְהַלְלוּךָ סֶּלָה.
בָּרוּךְ אַתָּה יי, הָאֵל הַקָּדוֹשׁ.*

*BETWEEN ROSH HASHANAH AND YOM KIPPUR CONCLUDE:

בָּרוּךְ אַתָּה יי, הַמֶּלֶךְ הַקָּדוֹשׁ.

You are holy, Your name is holy, and those who strive to be holy declare Your glory day by day.

*We praise You, Eternal One, the holy God.

*BETWEEN ROSH HASHANAH AND YOM KIPPUR CONCLUDE:

We praise You, Eternal One: You rule in holiness.

❖

FOR A MORNING OR AFTERNOON SERVICE

SANCTIFICATION   קדושה

נְקַדֵּשׁ אֶת־שִׁמְךָ בָּעוֹלָם, כְּשֵׁם שֶׁמַּקְדִּישִׁים אוֹתוֹ בִּשְׁמֵי
מָרוֹם, כַּכָּתוּב עַל־יַד נְבִיאֶךָ: וְקָרָא זֶה אֶל־זֶה וְאָמַר:

We sanctify Your name on earth, even as all things, to the ends of time and space, proclaim Your holiness, and in the words of the prophet we say:

קָדוֹשׁ, קָדוֹשׁ, קָדוֹשׁ יהוה צְבָאוֹת,
מְלֹא כָל־הָאָרֶץ כְּבוֹדוֹ.

Ka-dosh, ka-dosh, ka-dosh Adonai tz'va-oht,
m'lo chol ha-a-retz k'vo-doh.

Holy, holy, holy is the Eternal One, God of the Hosts of Heaven!
The whole earth is ablaze with Your glory!

לְעֻמָּתָם בָּרוּךְ יֹאמֵרוּ:

All being recounts Your praise:

בָּרוּךְ כְּבוֹד־יהוה מִמְּקוֹמוֹ.

Ba-ruch k'vod Adonai mim-ko-mo.

Praised be the glory of God in heaven and earth.

34

וּבְדִבְרֵי קָדְשְׁךָ כָּתוּב לֵאמֹר:

And this is Your sacred word:

יִמְלֹךְ יהוה לְעוֹלָם, אֱלֹהַיִךְ צִיּוֹן, לְדֹר וָדֹר. הַלְלוּיָהּ!

Yim-loch Adonai l'o-lam, eh-lo-ha-yich tzi-yon,
l'dor va-dor. Ha-l'lu-yah!

*The Eternal One shall reign for ever; your God, O Zion, from
generation to generation. Halleluyah!*

לְדוֹר וָדוֹר נַגִּיד גָּדְלֶךָ וּלְנֵצַח נְצָחִים קְדֻשָּׁתְךָ נַקְדִּישׁ.
וְשִׁבְחֲךָ, אֱלֹהֵינוּ, מִפִּינוּ לֹא יָמוּשׁ לְעוֹלָם וָעֶד.
*בָּרוּךְ אַתָּה יי, הָאֵל הַקָּדוֹשׁ.

*BETWEEN ROSH HASHANAH AND YOM KIPPUR CONCLUDE:
בָּרוּךְ אַתָּה יי, הַמֶּלֶךְ הַקָּדוֹשׁ.

To all generations we will make known Your greatness, and to
all eternity proclaim Your holiness. Your praise, O God, shall
never depart from our lips.

*We praise You, Eternal One, the holy God.

*BETWEEN ROSH HASHANAH AND YOM KIPPUR CONCLUDE:

We praise You, Eternal One: You rule in holiness.

❖ ❖

All are seated

35

INTERMEDIATE AND CONCLUDING BLESSINGS

Eternal Source of knowledge, You have endowed us with reason and understanding. We pray now for the light of Your truth, for insight into Your ways, and for the strength to banish from our hearts every desire and thought of evil.

> *Forgive our sins, pardon our failings, and help us to remove suffering and sorrow from our midst.*

May those who have lost their way come again to know Your love, and turn to You in newness of heart; and let those who love goodness and do justly rejoice in the knowledge of Your favor.

> *Bless our land with plenty and our nation with peace. May righteousness abide with us, and virtue bring us happiness. We praise You, Eternal God: You hearken to prayer.*

Eternal One, Creator of all the world, You have blessed us with noble powers: teach us to make wise use of them. You have called us to be Your partners in the work of creation, and we thank You for the power to choose a life devoted to Your service, dedicated to the well-being of those around us. May all that we do help to make Your majestic presence on earth a reality to all humankind.

> *May all peoples together find their way to establish peace on earth. Let them cultivate that good will, which alone can bring enduring peace.*

Let the nations realize that the triumphs of war turn to ashes, that justice and right are better than conquest and dominion.

> *May they come to see that it is not by might nor by power, but by Your spirit that life prevails.*

❖ ❖

MEDITATION

❖ ❖

יִהְיוּ לְרָצוֹן אִמְרֵי־פִי וְהֶגְיוֹן לִבִּי לְפָנֶיךָ, יהוה, צוּרִי וְגֹאֲלִי.

May the words of my mouth, and the meditations of my heart,
be acceptable to You, O God, my Rock and my Redeemer.

עֹשֶׂה שָׁלוֹם בִּמְרוֹמָיו, הוּא יַעֲשֶׂה שָׁלוֹם עָלֵינוּ וְעַל־כָּל־
יִשְׂרָאֵל, וְאִמְרוּ: אָמֵן.

O-seh sha-lom bim-ro-mav, hu ya-a-seh sha-lom a-lei-nu v'al kol
Yis-ra-eil, v'im-ru: A-mein.

May the One who causes peace to reign in the high heavens let
peace descend on us, on all Israel, and all the world.

Torah Service begins on page 68
Service at a House of Mourning begins on page 88
Aleinu is on page 74 or 77

37

Evening or Morning Service II

Infinite One, Your greatness surpasses our understanding, yet at times we feel Your nearness.

The signs of Your presence overwhelm us; flooded by awe and wonder, still we feel within us a kinship with the divine.

And so we turn to You, looking at the world about us, and inward to the world within us, there to find You, and from Your presence gain life and strength.

The Sh'ma and Its Blessings שמע וברכותיה

בָּרְכוּ אֶת־יי הַמְבֹרָךְ!

Praise the One to whom our praise is due!

בָּרוּךְ יי הַמְבֹרָךְ לְעוֹלָם וָעֶד!

Ba-ruch Adonai ha-m'vo-rach l'o-lam va-ed!

Praised be the One to whom our praise is due, now and for ever!

CREATION

EVENING

MORNING

בָּרוּךְ אַתָּה יי, אֱלֹהֵינוּ מֶלֶךְ
הָעוֹלָם, אֲשֶׁר בִּדְבָרוֹ
מַעֲרִיב עֲרָבִים, בְּחׇכְמָה
פּוֹתֵחַ שְׁעָרִים, וּבִתְבוּנָה
מְשַׁנֶּה עִתִּים, וּמַחֲלִיף אֶת־

בָּרוּךְ אַתָּה יי, אֱלֹהֵינוּ מֶלֶךְ
הָעוֹלָם, יוֹצֵר אוֹר וּבוֹרֵא
חֹשֶׁךְ, עֹשֶׂה שָׁלוֹם וּבוֹרֵא
אֶת־הַכֹּל. הַמֵּאִיר לָאָרֶץ
וְלַדָּרִים עָלֶיהָ בְּרַחֲמִים,

38

וּבְטוּבוֹ מְחַדֵּשׁ בְּכָל־יוֹם
תָּמִיד מַעֲשֵׂה בְרֵאשִׁית.
מָה רַבּוּ מַעֲשֶׂיךָ יְיָ! כֻּלָּם
בְּחָכְמָה עָשִׂיתָ, מָלְאָה
הָאָרֶץ קִנְיָנֶךָ. תִּתְבָּרַךְ, יְיָ
אֱלֹהֵינוּ, עַל־שֶׁבַח מַעֲשֵׂה
יָדֶיךָ, וְעַל־מְאוֹרֵי־אוֹר
שֶׁעָשִׂיתָ: יְפָאֲרוּךָ. סֶלָה.
בָּרוּךְ אַתָּה יְיָ, יוֹצֵר
הַמְּאוֹרוֹת.

הַזְּמַנִּים, וּמְסַדֵּר אֶת־
הַכּוֹכָבִים בְּמִשְׁמְרוֹתֵיהֶם
בָּרָקִיעַ כִּרְצוֹנוֹ. בּוֹרֵא יוֹם
וָלַיְלָה, גּוֹלֵל אוֹר מִפְּנֵי
חֹשֶׁךְ וְחֹשֶׁךְ מִפְּנֵי אוֹר,
וּמַעֲבִיר יוֹם וּמֵבִיא לַיְלָה,
וּמַבְדִּיל בֵּין יוֹם וּבֵין לַיְלָה,
יְיָ צְבָאוֹת שְׁמוֹ. אֵל חַי
וְקַיָּם, תָּמִיד יִמְלוֹךְ עָלֵינוּ
לְעוֹלָם וָעֶד! בָּרוּךְ אַתָּה יְיָ,
הַמַּעֲרִיב עֲרָבִים.

° Heaven and earth, O God, are the work of Your hands. The roaring seas and the life within them issue forth from Your creative will. The universe is one vast wonder proclaiming Your wisdom and singing Your greatness.

The mysteries of life and death, of growth and decay, alike display the miracle of Your creative power. God of life, the whole universe is Your dwelling-place, all being a hymn to Your glory!

REVELATION

MORNING

אַהֲבָה רַבָּה אֲהַבְתָּנוּ, יְיָ
אֱלֹהֵינוּ, חֶמְלָה גְדוֹלָה וִיתֵרָה
חָמַלְתָּ עָלֵינוּ. אָבִינוּ מַלְכֵּנוּ,
בַּעֲבוּר אֲבוֹתֵינוּ וְאִמּוֹתֵינוּ
שֶׁבָּטְחוּ בְךָ וַתְּלַמְּדֵם חֻקֵּי
חַיִּים, כֵּן תְּחָנֵּנוּ וּתְלַמְּדֵנוּ.

EVENING

אַהֲבַת עוֹלָם בֵּית יִשְׂרָאֵל
עַמְּךָ אָהָבְתָּ. תּוֹרָה וּמִצְוֹת,
חֻקִּים וּמִשְׁפָּטִים אוֹתָנוּ
לִמַּדְתָּ. עַל־כֵּן, יְיָ אֱלֹהֵינוּ,
בְּשָׁכְבֵּנוּ וּבְקוּמֵנוּ נָשִׂיחַ
בְּחֻקֶּיךָ, וְנִשְׂמַח בְּדִבְרֵי

אָבִינוּ, הָאָב הָרַחֲמָן, הַמְרַחֵם, רַחֵם עָלֵינוּ וְתֵן בְּלִבֵּנוּ לְהָבִין וּלְהַשְׂכִּיל, לִשְׁמֹעַ לִלְמֹד וּלְלַמֵּד, לִשְׁמֹר וְלַעֲשׂוֹת וּלְקַיֵּם אֶת־כָּל־דִּבְרֵי תַלְמוּד תּוֹרָתֶךָ בְּאַהֲבָה.

תוֹרָתְךָ וּבְמִצְוֹתֶיךָ לְעוֹלָם וָעֶד. כִּי הֵם חַיֵּינוּ וְאֹרֶךְ יָמֵינוּ, וּבָהֶם נֶהְגֶּה יוֹמָם וָלָיְלָה. וְאַהֲבָתְךָ אַל־תָּסוּר מִמֶּנּוּ לְעוֹלָמִים! בָּרוּךְ אַתָּה יי, אוֹהֵב עַמּוֹ יִשְׂרָאֵל.

וְהָאֵר עֵינֵינוּ בְּתוֹרָתֶךָ, וְדַבֵּק לִבֵּנוּ בְּמִצְוֹתֶיךָ, וְיַחֵד לְבָבֵנוּ לְאַהֲבָה וּלְיִרְאָה אֶת־שְׁמֶךָ. וְלֹא־נֵבוֹשׁ לְעוֹלָם וָעֶד, כִּי בְשֵׁם קָדְשְׁךָ הַגָּדוֹל וְהַנּוֹרָא בָּטָחְנוּ. נָגִילָה וְנִשְׂמְחָה בִּישׁוּעָתֶךָ, כִּי אֵל פּוֹעֵל יְשׁוּעוֹת אָתָּה, וּבָנוּ בָחַרְתָּ וְקֵרַבְתָּנוּ לְשִׁמְךָ הַגָּדוֹל סֶלָה בֶּאֱמֶת, לְהוֹדוֹת לְךָ וּלְיַחֶדְךָ בְּאַהֲבָה. בָּרוּךְ אַתָּה יי, הַבּוֹחֵר בְּעַמּוֹ יִשְׂרָאֵל בְּאַהֲבָה.

° In the human heart, too, You reign supreme. Above the storms of passion and hate that shake our world, we hear Your voice proclaim the law of justice and love.

May our eyes be open to Your truth, our spirits alive to Your teaching, our hearts united to serve You.

May we find the will to consecrate ourselves anew to the task of all the generations: to speed the dawn of a new day when all will be united in friendship and peace, and with one accord acclaim You their Eternal God.

❖ ❖

שְׁמַע יִשְׂרָאֵל: יהוה אֱלֹהֵינוּ, יהוה אֶחָד!

Sh'ma Yis-ra-eil: Adonai Eh-lo-hei-nu, Adonai Eh-chad!

Hear, O Israel: the Eternal One is our God,
the Eternal God alone!

בָּרוּךְ שֵׁם כְּבוֹד מַלְכוּתוֹ לְעוֹלָם וָעֶד!

Ba-ruch sheim k'vod mal-chu-toh l'o-lam va-ed!

Blessed is God's glorious majesty for ever and ever!

All are seated

וְאָהַבְתָּ אֵת יְהֹוָה אֱלֹהֶיךָ בְּכָל־לְבָבְךָ וּבְכָל־נַפְשְׁךָ
וּבְכָל־מְאֹדֶךָ: וְהָיוּ הַדְּבָרִים הָאֵלֶּה אֲשֶׁר אָנֹכִי מְצַוְּךָ
הַיּוֹם עַל־לְבָבֶךָ: וְשִׁנַּנְתָּם לְבָנֶיךָ וְדִבַּרְתָּ בָּם בְּשִׁבְתְּךָ
בְּבֵיתֶךָ וּבְלֶכְתְּךָ בַדֶּרֶךְ וּבְשָׁכְבְּךָ וּבְקוּמֶךָ: וּקְשַׁרְתָּם
לְאוֹת עַל־יָדֶךָ וְהָיוּ לְטֹטָפֹת בֵּין עֵינֶיךָ: וּכְתַבְתָּם
עַל־מְזֻזֹת בֵּיתֶךָ וּבִשְׁעָרֶיךָ:

V'a-hav-ta et Adonai Eh-lo-heh-cha b'chol l'va-v'cha u-v'chol naf-sh'cha u-v'chol m'o-deh-cha. V'ha-yu ha-d'va-rim ha-ei-leh a-sher a-no-chi m'tza-v'cha ha-yom al l'va-veh-cha. V'shi-nan-tam l'va-neh-cha v'di-bar-ta bam b'shiv-t'cha b'vei-teh-cha u-v'lech-t'cha va-deh-rech u-v'shoch-b'cha u-v'ku-meh-cha. U-k'shar-tam l'oht al ya-deh-cha v'ha-yu l'toh-ta-foht bein ei-neh-cha; u-ch'tav-tam al m'zu-zoht bei-teh-cha u-vi-sh'a-reh-cha.

You shall love the Eternal One, your God, with all your heart, with all your mind, with all your being. Set these words, which I command you this day, upon your heart. Teach them faithfully to your children; speak of them in your home and on your way, when you lie down and when you rise up. Bind them as a sign upon your hand; let them be a symbol before your eyes; inscribe them on the doorposts of your house, and on your gates.

לְמַעַן תִּזְכְּרוּ וַעֲשִׂיתֶם אֶת־כָּל־מִצְוֹתָי וִהְיִיתֶם קְדֹשִׁים
לֵאלֹהֵיכֶם: אֲנִי יְהֹוָה אֱלֹהֵיכֶם אֲשֶׁר הוֹצֵאתִי אֶתְכֶם
מֵאֶרֶץ מִצְרַיִם לִהְיוֹת לָכֶם לֵאלֹהִים אֲנִי יְהֹוָה אֱלֹהֵיכֶם:

L'ma-an tiz-k'ru va-a-si-tem et kol mitz-vo-tai, vi-h'yi-tem k'doh-shim lei-lo-hei-chem. A-ni Adonai Eh-lo-hei-chem a-sher ho-tzei-ti et chem mei-eh-retz mitz-ra-yim li-h'yoht la-chem lei-lo-him. A-ni Adonai Eh-lo-hei-chem.

Be mindful of all My Mitzvot, and do them: so shall you consecrate yourselves to your God. I am your Eternal God who led you out of Egypt to be your God; I am your Eternal God.

REDEMPTION גְּאוּלָה

EVENING

אֱמֶת וֶאֱמוּנָה כָּל־זֹאת, וְקַיָּם
עָלֵינוּ כִּי הוּא יְיָ אֱלֹהֵינוּ וְאֵין
זוּלָתוֹ, וַאֲנַחְנוּ יִשְׂרָאֵל עַמּוֹ.
הַפּוֹדֵנוּ מִיַּד מְלָכִים, מַלְכֵּנוּ
הַגּוֹאֲלֵנוּ מִכַּף כָּל־הֶעָרִיצִים.
הָעֹשֶׂה גְדֹלוֹת עַד אֵין חֵקֶר,
וְנִפְלָאוֹת עַד־אֵין מִסְפָּר.
הַשָּׂם נַפְשֵׁנוּ בַּחַיִּים, וְלֹא־נָתַן
לַמּוֹט רַגְלֵנוּ. הָעֹשֶׂה לָנוּ
נִסִּים בְּפַרְעֹה, אוֹתוֹת
וּמוֹפְתִים בְּאַדְמַת בְּנֵי חָם.
וַיּוֹצֵא אֶת־עַמּוֹ יִשְׂרָאֵל
מִתּוֹכָם לְחֵרוּת עוֹלָם. וְרָאוּ
בָנָיו וּבְנוֹתָיו גְּבוּרָתוֹ; שִׁבְּחוּ
וְהוֹדוּ לִשְׁמוֹ. וּמַלְכוּתוֹ
בְּרָצוֹן קִבְּלוּ עֲלֵיהֶם. מֹשֶׁה
וּמִרְיָם וּבְנֵי יִשְׂרָאֵל לְךָ עָנוּ
שִׁירָה בְּשִׂמְחָה רַבָּה, וְאָמְרוּ
כֻלָּם:

MORNING

עַל־הָרִאשׁוֹנִים וְעַל־
הָאַחֲרוֹנִים דָּבָר טוֹב וְקַיָּם
לְעוֹלָם וָעֶד. אֱמֶת וֶאֱמוּנָה,
חֹק וְלֹא יַעֲבוֹר. אֱמֶת שָׁאַתָּה
הוּא יְיָ אֱלֹהֵינוּ וֵאלֹהֵי
אֲבוֹתֵינוּ וְאִמּוֹתֵינוּ, מַלְכֵּנוּ
מֶלֶךְ אֲבוֹתֵינוּ וְאִמּוֹתֵינוּ,
גּוֹאֲלֵנוּ גּוֹאֵל אֲבוֹתֵינוּ
וְאִמּוֹתֵינוּ, יוֹצְרֵנוּ צוּר
יְשׁוּעָתֵנוּ. פּוֹדֵנוּ וּמַצִּילֵנוּ
מֵעוֹלָם הוּא שְׁמֶךָ, אֵין
אֱלֹהִים זוּלָתֶךָ. עֶזְרַת
אֲבוֹתֵינוּ וְאִמּוֹתֵינוּ אַתָּה הוּא
מֵעוֹלָם, מָגֵן וּמוֹשִׁיעַ לִבְנֵיהֶם
וְלִבְנוֹתֵיהֶם אַחֲרֵיהֶם בְּכָל־
דּוֹר וָדוֹר. בְּרוּם עוֹלָם
מוֹשָׁבֶךָ וּמִשְׁפָּטֶיךָ, וְצִדְקָתְךָ
עַד אַפְסֵי־אָרֶץ. אַשְׁרֵי אִישׁ
שֶׁיִּשְׁמַע לְמִצְוֹתֶיךָ וְתוֹרָתְךָ
וּדְבָרְךָ יָשִׂים עַל־לִבּוֹ.

42

° Infinite God, Creator and Redeemer of all being, You are Most High, Most Near. In all generations we have cried out to You; we have put our trust in You, we have borne witness to Your love before the nations! O now let Your light and Your love appear to us and lead us; bring us to Your holy mountain.

> *Then, though earth itself should shake, though the mountains fall into the heart of the sea, though its waters thunder and rage, though the winds lift its waves to the very vault of heaven, we shall not despair.*

We shall not lose hope, for You are with us; we shall rejoice in Your deliverance. Then shall we know You, our Redeemer and our God, and in the shadow of Your wings we shall sing with joy:

מִי־כָמְכָה בָּאֵלִם, יהוה? מִי כָּמְכָה, נֶאְדָּר בַּקֹּדֶשׁ,
נוֹרָא תְהִלֹּת, עֹשֵׂה פֶלֶא?

Mi cha-mo-cha ba-ei-lim, Adonai? Mi ka-mo-cha, neh-dar ba-ko-desh, no-ra t'hi-loht, o-sei feh-leh?

EVENING	MORNING

מַלְכוּתְךָ רָאוּ בָנֶיךָ, בּוֹקֵעַ יָם
לִפְנֵי מֹשֶׁה; זֶה אֵלִי! עָנוּ
וְאָמְרוּ: יהוה יִמְלֹךְ לְעֹלָם
וָעֶד!

שִׁירָה חֲדָשָׁה שִׁבְּחוּ גְאוּלִים
לְשִׁמְךָ עַל־שְׂפַת הַיָּם; יַחַד
כֻּלָּם הוֹדוּ וְהִמְלִיכוּ וְאָמְרוּ:
"יי יִמְלֹךְ לְעוֹלָם וָעֶד!"

וְנֶאֱמַר: כִּי פָדָה יי אֶת־יַעֲקֹב,
וּגְאָלוֹ מִיַּד חָזָק מִמֶּנּוּ.
בָּרוּךְ אַתָּה יי, גָּאַל יִשְׂרָאֵל.

צוּר יִשְׂרָאֵל, קוּמָה בְּעֶזְרַת
יִשְׂרָאֵל, וּפְדֵה כִנְאֻמֶךָ יְהוּדָה
וְיִשְׂרָאֵל. גֹּאֲלֵנוּ יי צְבָאוֹת
שְׁמוֹ, קְדוֹשׁ יִשְׂרָאֵל.
בָּרוּךְ אַתָּה, יי, גָּאַל יִשְׂרָאֵל.

43

Who is like You, Eternal One, among the gods that are worshipped? Who is like You, majestic in holiness, awesome in splendor, doing wonders?

When Your children perceived Your power they exclaimed: "This is my God!" "The Eternal One will reign for ever and ever!"

❖ ❖

FOR AN EVENING SERVICE

DIVINE PROVIDENCE   הַשְׁכִּיבֵנוּ

הַשְׁכִּיבֵנוּ, יי אֱלֹהֵינוּ, לְשָׁלוֹם, וְהַעֲמִידֵנוּ, מַלְכֵּנוּ, לְחַיִּים.
וּפְרוֹשׂ עָלֵינוּ סֻכַּת שְׁלוֹמֶךָ, וְתַקְּנֵנוּ בְּעֵצָה טוֹבָה מִלְּפָנֶיךָ,
וְהוֹשִׁיעֵנוּ לְמַעַן שְׁמֶךָ, וְהָגֵן בַּעֲדֵנוּ. וְהָסֵר מֵעָלֵינוּ אוֹיֵב,
דֶּבֶר וְחֶרֶב וְרָעָב וְיָגוֹן; וְהָסֵר שָׂטָן מִלְּפָנֵינוּ וּמֵאַחֲרֵינוּ,
וּבְצֵל כְּנָפֶיךָ תַּסְתִּירֵנוּ, כִּי אֵל שׁוֹמְרֵנוּ וּמַצִּילֵנוּ אָתָּה,
כִּי אֵל מֶלֶךְ חַנּוּן וְרַחוּם אָתָּה. וּשְׁמוֹר צֵאתֵנוּ וּבוֹאֵנוּ
לְחַיִּים וּלְשָׁלוֹם, מֵעַתָּה וְעַד עוֹלָם.

בָּרוּךְ אַתָּה יי, שׁוֹמֵר עַמּוֹ יִשְׂרָאֵל לָעַד.

° Let there be love and understanding among us; let home and friendship be our shelter from life's storms. Eternal God, help us to walk with good companions, to live with hope in our hearts and eternity in our thoughts, that we may lie down in peace and rise up to find our hearts waiting to do Your will.

We praise You, Eternal One, Guardian of Israel,
whose love gives light to all the world.

44

All rise

T'filah תפלה

אֲדֹנָי, שְׂפָתַי תִּפְתָּח וּפִי יַגִּיד תְּהִלָּתֶךָ.

Eternal God, open my lips, that my mouth may declare Your glory.

GOD OF ALL GENERATIONS   אבות ואמהות

בָּרוּךְ אַתָּה יי, אֱלֹהֵינוּ וֵאלֹהֵי אֲבוֹתֵינוּ וְאִמּוֹתֵינוּ:
אֱלֹהֵי אַבְרָהָם, אֱלֹהֵי יִצְחָק, וֵאלֹהֵי יַעֲקֹב.
אֱלֹהֵי שָׂרָה, אֱלֹהֵי רִבְקָה, אֱלֹהֵי לֵאָה, וֵאלֹהֵי רָחֵל.
הָאֵל הַגָּדוֹל הַגִּבּוֹר וְהַנּוֹרָא, אֵל עֶלְיוֹן, גּוֹמֵל חֲסָדִים
טוֹבִים וְקוֹנֵה הַכֹּל, וְזוֹכֵר חַסְדֵי אָבוֹת וְאִמָּהוֹת,
וּמֵבִיא גְאֻלָּה לִבְנֵי בְנֵיהֶם, לְמַעַן שְׁמוֹ בְּאַהֲבָה.

BETWEEN ROSH HASHANAH AND YOM KIPPUR ADD:

זָכְרֵנוּ לְחַיִּים, מֶלֶךְ חָפֵץ בַּחַיִּים,
וְכָתְבֵנוּ בְּסֵפֶר הַחַיִּים, לְמַעַנְךָ אֱלֹהִים חַיִּים.

מֶלֶךְ עוֹזֵר וּמוֹשִׁיעַ וּמָגֵן.
בָּרוּךְ אַתָּה יי, מָגֵן אַבְרָהָם וְעֶזְרַת שָׂרָה.

Ba-ruch a-ta Adonai, Eh-lo-hei-nu vei-lo-hei a-vo-tei-nu v'i-mo-tei-nu:
Eh-lo-hei Av-ra-ham, Eh-lo-hei Yitz-chak, vei-lo-hei Ya-a-kov. Eh-lo-
hei Sa-rah, Eh-lo-hei Riv-kah, Eh-lo-hei Lei-ah, vei-lo-hei Ra-cheil.
Ha-eil ha-ga-dol ha-gi-bor v'ha-no-ra, Eil el-yon. Go-meil cha-sa-dim
toh-vim, v'ko-nei ha-kol, v'zo-cheir chas-dei a-voht v'i-ma-hoht,
u-mei-vi g'u-la li-v'nei v'nei-hem, l'ma-an sh'mo, b'a-ha-va.

BETWEEN ROSH HASHANAH AND YOM KIPPUR ADD:

Zoch'rei-nu l'cha-yim, meh-lech cha-feitz ba-cha-yim,
v'cho-t'vei-nu b'sei-fer ha-cha-yim, l'ma-an-cha Eh-lo-him cha-yim.

Meh-lech o-zeir u-mo-shi-a u-ma-gein.
Ba-ruch a-ta Adonai, ma-gein Av-ra-ham v'ez-rat Sa-rah.

° God of ages past and future, God of this day,
as You were with our mothers and fathers, be with us as well.
> *As You strengthened them, strengthen us.*

As you were their Guide, be ours as well.
> *Grant that we too may be bearers of Your teaching,*
> *teachers of Your truth.*

Then our tradition shall endure, and Israel live; from mother and
father to daughter and son, and all who follow them.
> *May students of Torah become teachers,*
> *that the people and its tradition endure.*
> *The people and its tradition will live.*

GOD'S POWER _____ גבורות

אַתָּה גִבּוֹר לְעוֹלָם, אֲדֹנָי, מְחַיֵּה הַכֹּל אַתָּה, רַב לְהוֹשִׁיעַ.
מְכַלְכֵּל חַיִּים בְּחֶסֶד, מְחַיֵּה הַכֹּל בְּרַחֲמִים רַבִּים. סוֹמֵךְ
נוֹפְלִים, וְרוֹפֵא חוֹלִים, וּמַתִּיר אֲסוּרִים, וּמְקַיֵּם אֱמוּנָתוֹ
לִישֵׁנֵי עָפָר. מִי כָמוֹךָ בַּעַל גְּבוּרוֹת, וּמִי דוֹמֶה לָּךְ, מֶלֶךְ
מֵמִית וּמְחַיֶּה וּמַצְמִיחַ יְשׁוּעָה?

BETWEEN ROSH HASHANAH AND YOM KIPPUR ADD:

מִי כָמוֹךָ, אֵל הָרַחֲמִים, זוֹכֵר יְצוּרָיו לְחַיִּים בְּרַחֲמִים?

וְנֶאֱמָן אַתָּה לְהַחֲיוֹת הַכֹּל. בָּרוּךְ אַתָּה יי, מְחַיֵּה הַכֹּל.

A-ta gi-bor l'o-lam, Adonai, m'cha-yei ha-kol a-ta, rav l'ho-shi-a.
M'chal-keil cha-yim b'cheh-sed, m'cha-yei ha-kol b'ra-cha-mim ra-
bim. So-meich no-f'lim, v'ro-fei cho-lim, u-ma-tir a-su-rim, u-m'ka-
yeim eh-mu-na-toh li-shei-nei a-far. Mi cha-mo-cha ba-al g'vu-roht,
u-mi doh-meh lach, meh-lech mei-mit u-m'cha-yeh u-matz-mi-ach
y'shu-a?

46

BETWEEN ROSH HASHANAH AND YOM KIPPUR ADD:

Mi cha-mo-cha, Eil ha-ra-cha-mim, zo-cheir y'tzu-rav l'cha-yim
b'ra-cha-mim?

V'neh-eh-man a-ta l'ha-cha-yoht ha-kol. Ba-ruch a-ta Adonai,
m'cha-yei ha-kol.

° Your might, O God, is everlasting;
Help us to use our strength for good.

You are the Source of life and blessing;
Help us to choose life for ourselves and our children.

You are the Support of the falling;
Help us to lift up the fallen.

You are the Author of freedom;
Help us to set free the captive;

You are our Hope in death as in life;
Help us to keep faith with those who sleep in the dust.

Your might, O God, is everlasting;
Help us to use our strength for good.

❖ ❖

FOR AN EVENING SERVICE

THE HOLINESS OF GOD   קְדוּשַׁת הַשֵּׁם

אַתָּה קָדוֹשׁ וְשִׁמְךָ קָדוֹשׁ, וּקְדוֹשִׁים בְּכָל־יוֹם יְהַלְלוּךָ סֶּלָה.
*בָּרוּךְ אַתָּה יי, הָאֵל הַקָּדוֹשׁ.

*BETWEEN ROSH HASHANAH AND YOM KIPPUR CONCLUDE:
בָּרוּךְ אַתָּה יי, הַמֶּלֶךְ הַקָּדוֹשׁ.

47

You are holy, Your name is holy, and those who strive to be holy declare Your glory day by day.

*We praise You, Eternal One, the holy God.

*BETWEEN ROSH HASHANAH AND YOM KIPPUR CONCLUDE:

We praise You, Eternal One: You rule in holiness.

❖

FOR A MORNING OR AFTERNOON SERVICE

SANCTIFICATION   קְדוּשָׁה

נְקַדֵּשׁ אֶת־שִׁמְךָ בָּעוֹלָם, כְּשֵׁם שֶׁמַּקְדִּישִׁים אוֹתוֹ בִּשְׁמֵי
מָרוֹם, כַּכָּתוּב עַל־יַד נְבִיאֶךָ: וְקָרָא זֶה אֶל־זֶה וְאָמַר:

We sanctify Your name on earth, even as all things, to the ends of time and space, proclaim Your holiness, and in the words of the prophet we say:

קָדוֹשׁ, קָדוֹשׁ, קָדוֹשׁ יהוה צְבָאוֹת,
מְלֹא כָל־הָאָרֶץ כְּבוֹדוֹ.

Ka-dosh, ka-dosh, ka-dosh Adonai tz'va-oht,
m'lo chol ha-a-retz k'vo-doh.

*Holy, holy, holy is the Eternal One, God of the Hosts of Heaven!
The whole earth is ablaze with Your glory!*

לְעֻמָּתָם בָּרוּךְ יֹאמֵרוּ:

All being recounts Your praise:

בָּרוּךְ כְּבוֹד־יהוה מִמְּקוֹמוֹ.

Ba-ruch k'vod Adonai mim-ko-mo.

Praised be the glory of God in heaven and earth.

48

וּבְדִבְרֵי קָדְשְׁךָ כָּתוּב לֵאמֹר:

And this is Your sacred word:

יִמְלֹךְ יהוה לְעוֹלָם, אֱלֹהַיִךְ צִיּוֹן, לְדֹר וָדֹר. הַלְלוּיָהּ!

Yim-loch Adonai l'o-lam, eh-lo-ha-yich tzi-yon,
l'dor va-dor. Ha-l'lu-yah!

*The Eternal One shall reign for ever; your God, O Zion, from
generation to generation. Halleluyah!*

לְדוֹר וָדוֹר נַגִּיד גָּדְלֶךָ וּלְנֵצַח נְצָחִים קְדֻשָּׁתְךָ נַקְדִּישׁ.
וְשִׁבְחֲךָ, אֱלֹהֵינוּ, מִפִּינוּ לֹא יָמוּשׁ לְעוֹלָם וָעֶד.
*בָּרוּךְ אַתָּה יי, הָאֵל הַקָּדוֹשׁ.

*BETWEEN ROSH HASHANAH AND YOM KIPPUR CONCLUDE:
בָּרוּךְ אַתָּה יי, הַמֶּלֶךְ הַקָּדוֹשׁ.

To all generations we will make known Your greatness, and to
all eternity proclaim Your holiness. Your praise, O God, shall
never depart from our lips.

*We praise You, Eternal One, the holy God.

*BETWEEN ROSH HASHANAH AND YOM KIPPUR CONCLUDE:
We praise You, Eternal One: You rule in holiness.

All are seated

THE INTERMEDIATE BLESSINGS   בקשות

We give thanks for the divine flame that glows within, the gift
of reason that enables us to search after knowledge.

Blessed is the Eternal Source of wisdom and knowledge.

49

May our pride of intellect never be an idol turning us away from feeling wonder and awe. And as we grow in knowledge, may we remain aware that all our learning is but a handful of bright pebbles picked from the wide shore of the unknown.

Blessed is the One to whom all things are known.

May the beauty and mystery of the world move us to reverence and humility. Let the tree of knowledge bear good fruit for us and our children.

Blessed is the One from whom all blessings flow.

And let the consciousness of Your presence be the glory of our lives, making joyous our days and years.

Blessed is the One who hearkens to prayer.

❖ ❖

MEDITATION

❖ ❖

יִהְיוּ לְרָצוֹן אִמְרֵי־פִי וְהֶגְיוֹן לִבִּי לְפָנֶיךָ, יהוה, צוּרִי וְגֹאֲלִי.

May the words of my mouth, and the meditations of my heart, be acceptable to You, O God, my Rock and my Redeemer.

❖

עֹשֶׂה שָׁלוֹם בִּמְרוֹמָיו, הוּא יַעֲשֶׂה שָׁלוֹם עָלֵינוּ וְעַל־כָּל־
יִשְׂרָאֵל, וְאִמְרוּ: אָמֵן.

O-seh sha-lom bim-ro-mav, hu ya-a-seh sha-lom a-lei-nu v'al kol Yis-ra-eil, v'im-ru: A-mein.

May the One who causes peace to reign in the high heavens let peace descend on us, on all Israel, and all the world.

Torah Service begins on page 68

Service at a House of Mourning begins on page 88

Aleinu is on page 74 or 77

Evening or Morning Service III

You give meaning to our days, to our struggles and strivings. Without You we are lost, our lives empty. Then we turn to You! And then, in the stillness of the night and in the press of the crowd, Yours is the voice within that brings joy and peace.

We do not ask for a life of ease, for happiness without alloy. We ask only to be uncomplaining and unafraid. In our darkness be our light, and in our loneliness help us discover the many souls akin to our own. Give us strength to face life with courage, to draw blessing even from its discords and conflicts. Make us understand that life calls us not merely to enjoy the richness of the earth, but to exult in heights gained after the toil of climbing.

Let our darkness be dispelled by Your love, that we may rise above fear and failure, our steps sustained by faith. You give meaning to our days; You are our support and our trust.

All rise

The Sh'ma and Its Blessings שמע וברכותיה

בָּרְכוּ אֶת־יי הַמְבֹרָךְ!

Praise the One to whom our praise is due!

בָּרוּךְ יי הַמְבֹרָךְ לְעוֹלָם וָעֶד!

Ba-ruch Adonai ha-m'vo-rach l'o-lam va-ed!

Praised be the One to whom our praise is due, now and for ever!

CREATION AND REVELATION

בָּרוּךְ אַתָּה יי, אֱלֹהֵינוּ מֶלֶךְ הָעוֹלָם,
עֹשֶׂה מַעֲשֵׂה בְרֵאשִׁית.

We praise You, God of time and space,
Source of creation and its wonders.
You give light to the world and all the living.

בָּרוּךְ אַתָּה יי, אֱלֹהֵינוּ מֶלֶךְ הָעוֹלָם,
שֶׁכֹּחוֹ וּגְבוּרָתוֹ מָלֵא עוֹלָם.

We praise You, God of time and space,
whose power and might pervade the world.
How manifold are Your works, Eternal One;
in wisdom You have made them all.

בָּרוּךְ אַתָּה יי, אֱלֹהֵינוּ מֶלֶךְ הָעוֹלָם,
זוֹכֵר הַבְּרִית וְנֶאֱמָן בִּבְרִיתוֹ וְקַיָּם בְּמַאֲמָרוֹ.

We praise You, God of time and space. True to Your
word, You remember Your covenant with creation.
In Your goodness You renew the work of creation
continually, day by day.

בָּרוּךְ אַתָּה יי, אֱלֹהֵינוּ מֶלֶךְ הָעוֹלָם,
שֶׁנָּתַן מֵחָכְמָתוֹ לְבָשָׂר וָדָם.

We praise You, God of time and space,
for You share Your wisdom with flesh and blood.
Be gracious now to us, and teach us.
Guide us with compassion; show us how to know and
understand, to learn and teach: to uphold Your Torah
with love, and with love to hear Your words.

בָּרוּךְ אַתָּה יי, אֱלֹהֵינוּ מֶלֶךְ הָעוֹלָם,
אֲשֶׁר קִדְּשָׁנוּ בְּמִצְוֹתָיו וְצִוָּנוּ לַעֲסוֹק בְּדִבְרֵי תוֹרָה.

We praise You, God of time and space:
You hallow us with the Mitzvah of Torah
and invite us to immerse ourselves in its words.
Open our eyes with Your Teaching;
consecrate our hearts to Your Mitzvot;
and let the love and awe of Your name make us whole.

בָּרוּךְ אַתָּה יי, הַמְלַמֵּד תּוֹרָה לְעַמּוֹ יִשְׂרָאֵל.

We praise You, God of time and space,
Teacher of Torah to our people Israel.

בָּרוּךְ אַתָּה יי, הַבּוֹחֵר בְּעַמּוֹ יִשְׂרָאֵל בְּאַהֲבָה.

We praise You, Eternal One:
in love You have called Your people Israel to serve You.

❖ ❖

שְׁמַע יִשְׂרָאֵל: יהוה אֱלֹהֵינוּ, יהוה אֶחָד!

Sh'ma Yis-ra-eil: Adonai Eh-lo-hei-nu, Adonai Eh-chad!

Hear, O Israel: the Eternal One is our God,
the Eternal God alone!

בָּרוּךְ שֵׁם כְּבוֹד מַלְכוּתוֹ לְעוֹלָם וָעֶד!

Ba-ruch sheim k'vod mal-chu-toh l'o-lam va-ed!

Blessed is God's glorious majesty for ever and ever!

All are seated

וְאָהַבְתָּ אֵת יְהֹוָה אֱלֹהֶיךָ בְּכָל־לְבָבְךָ וּבְכָל־נַפְשְׁךָ
וּבְכָל־מְאֹדֶךָ: וְהָיוּ הַדְּבָרִים הָאֵלֶּה אֲשֶׁר אָנֹכִי מְצַוְּךָ
הַיּוֹם עַל־לְבָבֶךָ: וְשִׁנַּנְתָּם לְבָנֶיךָ וְדִבַּרְתָּ בָּם בְּשִׁבְתְּךָ
בְּבֵיתֶךָ וּבְלֶכְתְּךָ בַדֶּרֶךְ וּבְשָׁכְבְּךָ וּבְקוּמֶךָ: וּקְשַׁרְתָּם
לְאוֹת עַל־יָדֶךָ וְהָיוּ לְטֹטָפֹת בֵּין עֵינֶיךָ: וּכְתַבְתָּם
עַל־מְזוּזֹת בֵּיתֶךָ וּבִשְׁעָרֶיךָ:

V'a-hav-ta et Adonai Eh-lo-heh-cha b'chol l'va-v'cha u-v'chol naf-sh'cha u-v'chol m'o-deh-cha. V'ha-yu ha-d'va-rim ha-ei-leh a-sher a-no-chi m'tza-v'cha ha-yom al l'va-veh-cha. V'shi-nan-tam l'va-neh-cha v'di-bar-ta bam b'shiv-t'cha b'vei-teh-cha u-v'lech-t'cha va-deh-rech u-v'shoch-b'cha u-v'ku-meh-cha. U-k'shar-tam l'oht al ya-deh-cha v'ha-yu l'toh-ta-foht bein ei-neh-cha; u-ch'tav-tam al m'zu-zoht bei-teh-cha u-vi-sh'a-reh-cha.

> *You shall love the Eternal One, your God, with all your heart, with all your mind, with all your being. Set these words, which I command you this day, upon your heart. Teach them faithfully to your children; speak of them in your home and on your way, when you lie down and when you rise up. Bind them as a sign upon your hand; let them be a symbol before your eyes; inscribe them on the door-posts of your house, and on your gates.*

לְמַעַן תִּזְכְּרוּ וַעֲשִׂיתֶם אֶת־כָּל־מִצְוֹתָי וִהְיִיתֶם קְדֹשִׁים
לֵאלֹהֵיכֶם: אֲנִי יְהוָה אֱלֹהֵיכֶם אֲשֶׁר הוֹצֵאתִי אֶתְכֶם
מֵאֶרֶץ מִצְרַיִם לִהְיוֹת לָכֶם לֵאלֹהִים אֲנִי יְהוָה אֱלֹהֵיכֶם:

L'ma-an tiz-k'ru va-a-si-tem et kol mitz-vo-tai, vi-h'yi-tem k'doh-shim lei-lo-hei-chem. A-ni Adonai Eh-lo-hei-chem a-sher ho-tzei-ti et-chem mei-eh-retz mitz-ra-yim li-h'yoht la-chem lei-lo-him. A-ni Adonai Eh-lo-hei-chem.

> *Be mindful of all My Mitzvot, and do them: so shall you consecrate yourselves to your God. I am your Eternal God who led you out of Egypt to be your God; I am your Eternal God.*

REDEMPTION גאולה

EVENING   MORNING

עַל־הָרִאשׁוֹנִים וְעַל־
הָאַחֲרוֹנִים דָּבָר טוֹב וְקַיָּם
לְעוֹלָם וָעֶד. אֱמֶת וֶאֱמוּנָה,
חֹק וְלֹא יַעֲבוֹר. אֱמֶת שָׁאַתָּה
הוּא יי אֱלֹהֵינוּ וֵאלֹהֵי
אֲבוֹתֵינוּ וְאִמּוֹתֵינוּ, מַלְכֵּנוּ
מֶלֶךְ אֲבוֹתֵינוּ וְאִמּוֹתֵינוּ,
גּוֹאֲלֵנוּ גּוֹאֵל אֲבוֹתֵינוּ
וְאִמּוֹתֵינוּ, יוֹצְרֵנוּ צוּר
יְשׁוּעָתֵנוּ. פּוֹדֵנוּ וּמַצִּילֵנוּ
מֵעוֹלָם הוּא שְׁמֶךָ, אֵין
אֱלֹהִים זוּלָתֶךָ. עֶזְרַת
אֲבוֹתֵינוּ וְאִמּוֹתֵינוּ אַתָּה הוּא
מֵעוֹלָם, מָגֵן וּמוֹשִׁיעַ לִבְנֵיהֶם
וְלִבְנוֹתֵיהֶם אַחֲרֵיהֶם בְּכָל־
דּוֹר וָדוֹר. בְּרוּם עוֹלָם
מוֹשָׁבֶךָ וּמִשְׁפָּטֶיךָ, וְצִדְקָתְךָ
עַד אַפְסֵי־אָרֶץ. אַשְׁרֵי אִישׁ
שֶׁיִּשְׁמַע לְמִצְוֹתֶיךָ וְתוֹרָתְךָ
וּדְבָרְךָ יָשִׂים עַל־לִבּוֹ.

אֱמֶת וֶאֱמוּנָה כָּל־זֹאת, וְקַיָּם
עָלֵינוּ כִּי הוּא יי אֱלֹהֵינוּ וְאֵין
זוּלָתוֹ, וַאֲנַחְנוּ יִשְׂרָאֵל עַמּוֹ.
הַפּוֹדֵנוּ מִיַּד מְלָכִים, מַלְכֵּנוּ
הַגּוֹאֲלֵנוּ מִכַּף כָּל־הֶעָרִיצִים.
הָעֹשֶׂה גְדֹלוֹת עַד אֵין חֵקֶר,
וְנִפְלָאוֹת עַד־אֵין מִסְפָּר.
הַשָּׂם נַפְשֵׁנוּ בַּחַיִּים, וְלֹא־נָתַן
לַמּוֹט רַגְלֵנוּ. הָעֹשֶׂה לָּנוּ
נִסִּים בְּפַרְעֹה, אוֹתוֹת
וּמוֹפְתִים בְּאַדְמַת בְּנֵי חָם.
וַיּוֹצֵא אֶת־עַמּוֹ יִשְׂרָאֵל
מִתּוֹכָם לְחֵרוּת עוֹלָם. וְרָאוּ
בָנָיו וּבְנוֹתָיו גְּבוּרָתוֹ; שִׁבְּחוּ
וְהוֹדוּ לִשְׁמוֹ. וּמַלְכוּתוֹ
בְרָצוֹן קִבְּלוּ עֲלֵיהֶם. מֹשֶׁה
וּמִרְיָם וּבְנֵי יִשְׂרָאֵל לְךָ עָנוּ
שִׁירָה בְּשִׂמְחָה רַבָּה, וְאָמְרוּ
כֻלָּם:

° Eternal truth it is that You alone are God,
and there is none else.

*May all the world rejoice in Your love
and exult in Your justice.*

Let them beat their swords into plowshares;
Let them beat their spears into pruning-hooks.

Let nation not lift up sword against nation;
let them study war no more.

You shall not hate another in your heart;
you shall love your neighbor as yourself.

Let the stranger in your midst be to you as the native;
for you were strangers in the land of Egypt.

From the house of bondage we went forth to freedom,
and we sing in praise of Your name:

מִי־כָמֹכָה בָּאֵלִם, יהוה? מִי כָּמֹכָה, נֶאְדָּר בַּקֹּדֶשׁ,
נוֹרָא תְהִלֹּת, עֹשֵׂה פֶלֶא?

Mi cha-mo-cha ba-ei-lim, Adonai? Mi ka-mo-cha, neh-dar ba-ko-
desh, no-ra t'hi-loht, o-sei feh-leh?

EVENING	MORNING

MORNING

שִׁירָה חֲדָשָׁה שִׁבְּחוּ גְאוּלִים
לְשִׁמְךָ עַל־שְׂפַת הַיָּם; יַחַד
כֻּלָּם הוֹדוּ וְהִמְלִיכוּ וְאָמְרוּ:
"יי יִמְלֹךְ לְעוֹלָם וָעֶד"

צוּר יִשְׂרָאֵל, קוּמָה בְּעֶזְרַת
יִשְׂרָאֵל, וּפְדֵה כִנְאֻמֶךָ יְהוּדָה
וְיִשְׂרָאֵל. גֹּאֲלֵנוּ יי צְבָאוֹת
שְׁמוֹ, קְדוֹשׁ יִשְׂרָאֵל.
בָּרוּךְ אַתָּה, יי, גָּאַל יִשְׂרָאֵל.

EVENING

מַלְכוּתְךָ רָאוּ בָנֶיךָ, בּוֹקֵעַ יָם
לִפְנֵי מֹשֶׁה; זֶה אֵלִי! עָנוּ
וְאָמְרוּ: יהוה יִמְלֹךְ לְעֹלָם
וָעֶד!

וְנֶאֱמַר: כִּי פָדָה יי אֶת־יַעֲקֹב,
וּגְאָלוֹ מִיַּד חָזָק מִמֶּנּוּ.
בָּרוּךְ אַתָּה יי, גָּאַל יִשְׂרָאֵל.

Who is like You, Eternal One, among the gods that are worshipped? Who
is like You, majestic in holiness, awesome in splendor, doing wonders?

When Your children perceived Your power they exclaimed: "This is my
God!" "The Eternal One will reign for ever and ever!"

All rise

T'filah תפלה

GOD OF ALL GENERATIONS   אבות ואמהות

בָּרוּךְ אַתָּה יי, אֱלֹהֵינוּ וֵאלֹהֵי אֲבוֹתֵינוּ וְאִמּוֹתֵינוּ:
אֱלֹהֵי אַבְרָהָם, אֱלֹהֵי יִצְחָק, וֵאלֹהֵי יַעֲקֹב.
אֱלֹהֵי שָׂרָה, אֱלֹהֵי רִבְקָה, אֱלֹהֵי לֵאָה, וֵאלֹהֵי רָחֵל.
הָאֵל הַגָּדוֹל הַגִּבּוֹר וְהַנּוֹרָא, אֵל עֶלְיוֹן, קֹנֵה שָׁמַיִם וָאָרֶץ.

Ba-ruch a-ta Adonai, Eh-lo-hei-nu vei-lo-hei a-vo-tei-nu v'i-mo-tei-
nu: Eh-lo-hei Av-ra-ham, Eh-lo-hei Yitz-chak, vei-lo-hei Ya-a-kov.
Eh-lo-hei Sa-rah, Eh-lo-hei Riv-kah, Eh-lo-hei Lei-ah, vei-lo-hei Ra-
cheil. Ha-eil ha-ga-dol ha-gi-bor v'ha-no-ra, Eil el-yon, koh-nei sha-
ma-yim va-a-retz.

° God of all generations, of Abraham and Sarah, Rebekah and
Isaac, Leah, Rachel, and Jacob: be praised! Your wondrous creative power fills heaven and earth.

GOD'S POWER   גבורות

אַתָּה גִּבּוֹר לְעוֹלָם, אֲדֹנָי, מְחַיֵּה הַכֹּל אַתָּה, רַב לְהוֹשִׁיעַ.
מְכַלְכֵּל חַיִּים בְּחֶסֶד, מְחַיֵּה הַכֹּל בְּרַחֲמִים רַבִּים. סוֹמֵךְ
נוֹפְלִים, וְרוֹפֵא חוֹלִים, וּמַתִּיר אֲסוּרִים, וּמְקַיֵּם אֱמוּנָתוֹ
לִישֵׁנֵי עָפָר. מִי כָמוֹךָ בַּעַל גְּבוּרוֹת, וּמִי דוֹמֶה לָךְ, מֶלֶךְ
מֵמִית וּמְחַיֵּה וּמַצְמִיחַ יְשׁוּעָה?

BETWEEN ROSH HASHANAH AND YOM KIPPUR ADD:

מִי כָמוֹךָ, אֵל הָרַחֲמִים, זוֹכֵר יְצוּרָיו לְחַיִּים בְּרַחֲמִים?

וְנֶאֱמָן אַתָּה לְהַחֲיוֹת הַכֹּל. בָּרוּךְ אַתָּה יי, מְחַיֵּה הַכֹּל.

A-ta gi-bor l'o-lam, Adonai, m'cha-yei ha-kol a-ta, rav l'ho-shi-a.
M'chal-keil cha-yim b'cheh-sed, m'cha-yei ha-kol b'ra-cha-mim

ra-bim. So-meich no-f'lim, v'ro-fei cho-lim, u-ma-tir a-su-rim, u-m'ka-yeim eh-mu-na-toh li-shei-nei a-far. Mi cha-mo-cha ba-al g'vu-roht, u-mi doh-meh lach, meh-lech mei-mit u-m'cha-yeh u-matz-mi-ach y'shu-a?

BETWEEN ROSH HASHANAH AND YOM KIPPUR ADD:

Mi cha-mo-cha, Eil ha-ra-cha-mim, zo-cheir y'tzu-rav l'cha-yim b'ra-cha-mim?

V'neh-eh-man a-ta l'ha-cha-yoht ha-kol. Ba-ruch a-ta Adonai, m'cha-yei ha-kol.

° *For Your many blessings, O God, we give thanks. From You comes our life, and in Your great love You sustain it within us.*

You give strength to the weak, courage to those who are afraid, and light to all who dwell in darkness.

Source of all that we are and have, teach us to use our gifts in Your service, for the well-being of our nation and our world. Then will our lives give glory to Your name.

FOR AN EVENING SERVICE

THE HOLINESS OF GOD   קְדוּשַׁת הַשֵּׁם

אַתָּה קָדוֹשׁ וְשִׁמְךָ קָדוֹשׁ, וּקְדוֹשִׁים בְּכָל־יוֹם יְהַלְלוּךָ סֶּלָה.
*בָּרוּךְ אַתָּה יי, הָאֵל הַקָּדוֹשׁ.

*BETWEEN ROSH HASHANAH AND YOM KIPPUR CONCLUDE:

בָּרוּךְ אַתָּה יי, הַמֶּלֶךְ הַקָּדוֹשׁ.

You are holy, Your name is holy, and those who strive to be holy declare Your glory day by day.

*We praise You, Eternal One, the holy God.

*BETWEEN ROSH HASHANAH AND YOM KIPPUR CONCLUDE:

We praise You, Eternal One: You rule in holiness.

❖

FOR A MORNING OR AFTERNOON SERVICE

SANCTIFICATION   קדושה

נְקַדֵּשׁ אֶת־שִׁמְךָ בָּעוֹלָם, כְּשֵׁם שֶׁמַּקְדִּישִׁים אוֹתוֹ בִּשְׁמֵי
מָרוֹם, כַּכָּתוּב עַל־יַד נְבִיאֶךָ: וְקָרָא זֶה אֶל־זֶה וְאָמַר:

We sanctify Your name on earth, even as all things, to the ends
of time and space, proclaim Your holiness, and in the words of
the prophet we say:

קָדוֹשׁ, קָדוֹשׁ, קָדוֹשׁ יהוה צְבָאוֹת,
מְלֹא כָל־הָאָרֶץ כְּבוֹדוֹ.

Ka-dosh, ka-dosh, ka-dosh Adonai tz'va-oht,
m'lo chol ha-a-retz k'vo-doh.

*Holy, holy, holy is the Eternal One, God of the Hosts of Heaven!
The whole earth is ablaze with Your glory!*

לְעֻמָּתָם בָּרוּךְ יֹאמֵרוּ:

All being recounts Your praise:

בָּרוּךְ כְּבוֹד־יהוה מִמְּקוֹמוֹ.

Ba-ruch k'vod Adonai mim-ko-mo.

Praised be the glory of God in heaven and earth.

וּבְדִבְרֵי קָדְשְׁךָ כָּתוּב לֵאמֹר:

And this is Your sacred word:

יִמְלֹךְ יהוה לְעוֹלָם, אֱלֹהַיִךְ צִיּוֹן, לְדֹר וָדֹר. הַלְלוּיָהּ!

Yim-loch Adonai l'o-lam, eh-lo-ha-yich tzi-yon,
l'dor va-dor. Ha-l'lu-yah!

*The Eternal One shall reign for ever; your God, O Zion, from
generation to generation. Halleluyah!*

לְדוֹר וָדוֹר נַגִּיד גָּדְלֶךָ וּלְנֵצַח נְצָחִים קְדֻשָּׁתְךָ נַקְדִּישׁ.
וְשִׁבְחֲךָ, אֱלֹהֵינוּ, מִפִּינוּ לֹא יָמוּשׁ לְעוֹלָם וָעֶד.
*בָּרוּךְ אַתָּה יי, הָאֵל הַקָּדוֹשׁ.

*BETWEEN ROSH HASHANAH AND YOM KIPPUR CONCLUDE:

בָּרוּךְ אַתָּה יי, הַמֶּלֶךְ הַקָּדוֹשׁ.

To all generations we will make known Your greatness, and to
all eternity proclaim Your holiness. Your praise, O God, shall
never depart from our lips.

*We praise You, Eternal One, the holy God.

*BETWEEN ROSH HASHANAH AND YOM KIPPUR CONCLUDE:

We praise You, Eternal One: You rule in holiness.

All are seated

THE INTERMEDIATE BLESSINGS   בקשות

הֲבִינֵנוּ, יי אֱלֹהֵינוּ, לָדַעַת דְּרָכֶיךָ, וּמוֹל אֶת־לְבָבֵנוּ לְיִרְאָתֶךָ.
וְתִסְלַח לָנוּ לִהְיוֹת גְּאוּלִים; וְרַחֲקֵנוּ מִמַּכְאוֹב.
וְדַשְּׁנֵנוּ בִּנְאוֹת אַרְצֶךָ, וּנְפוּצוֹתֵינוּ מֵאַרְבַּע כַּנְפוֹת הָאָרֶץ
תְּקַבֵּץ. וְהַתּוֹעִים עַל־דַּעְתְּךָ יִשָּׁפֵטוּ; וְעַל־הָרְשָׁעָה תָּנִיף
יָדֶךָ. וְיִשְׂמְחוּ צַדִּיקִים בְּבִנְיַן עִירֶךָ, וּבְצִמְיחַת קֶרֶן יְשׁוּעָתֶךָ.
טֶרֶם נִקְרָא אַתָּה תַעֲנֶה. בָּרוּךְ אַתָּה יי, שׁוֹמֵעַ תְּפִלָּה.

Give us insight to understand Your ways,
and consecrate our hearts to revere You.
> *For our sins forgive us;*
> *from pain and sorrow deliver us.*

Bestow upon us Your earth's abundance,
and gather our exiles from earth's four corners.
> *To those who stray bring correction;*
> *upon the lawless place Your hand.*

Let the righteous rejoice in the building of Your city
and the flowering of Your redemption.
> *Before we call comes Your reply.*
> *We praise You, Eternal One: You hearken to prayer.*

THE CONCLUDING BLESSINGS   ברכות אחרונות

Let Your spirit rule this nation and its citizens, that their deeds
may be prompted by a love of justice and right, and bear fruit in
goodness and peace.
> *Bless our people with a love of righteousness.*

Teach us to work for the welfare of all, to diminish the evils that
beset us, and to enlarge our nation's virtues.
> *Bless our people with civic courage.*

Bless our striving to make real the dream of Your sovereign
rule, when we shall have put an end to the suffering we now
inflict on one another.
> *Bless our people with a vision of that rule on earth.*

For You have endowed us with noble powers; help us to use
them wisely, and with compassion.
> *Bless our people with a wise and feeling heart.*

You have given us freedom to choose between good and evil,
life and death. May we choose life and good, that our children
may inherit from us the blessings of dignity and freedom,
prosperity and peace.

❖ ❖

MEDITATION

❖ ❖

יִהְיוּ לְרָצוֹן אִמְרֵי־פִי וְהֶגְיוֹן לִבִּי לְפָנֶיךָ, יהוה, צוּרִי וְגֹאֲלִי.

May the words of my mouth, and the meditations of my heart,
be acceptable to You, O God, my Rock and my Redeemer.

❖

עֹשֶׂה שָׁלוֹם בִּמְרוֹמָיו, הוּא יַעֲשֶׂה שָׁלוֹם עָלֵינוּ וְעַל־כָּל־
יִשְׂרָאֵל, וְאִמְרוּ: אָמֵן.

O-seh sha-lom bim-ro-mav, hu ya-a-seh sha-lom a-lei-nu v'al kol
Yis-ra-eil, v'im-ru: A-mein.

May the One who causes peace to reign in the high heavens let
peace descend on us, on all Israel, and all the world.

Torah Service begins on page 68
Service at a House of Mourning begins on page 88
Aleinu is on page 74 or 77

Afternoon Service   מנחה

Ashrei   אשרי

אַשְׁרֵי יוֹשְׁבֵי בֵיתֶךָ; עוֹד יְהַלְלוּךָ סֶּלָה.

אַשְׁרֵי הָעָם שֶׁכָּכָה לּוֹ; אַשְׁרֵי הָעָם שֶׁיהוה אֱלֹהָיו.

Happy are those who dwell in Your house;

they will sing your praise for ever.

Happy the people to whom such blessing falls;

Happy the people of the Eternal God.

Psalm 145

תְּהִלָּה לְדָוִד.

אֲרוֹמִמְךָ, אֱלוֹהַי הַמֶּלֶךְ, וַאֲבָרְכָה שִׁמְךָ לְעוֹלָם וָעֶד.

בְּכָל־יוֹם אֲבָרְכֶךָּ, וַאֲהַלְלָה שִׁמְךָ לְעוֹלָם וָעֶד.

I will exalt You, my Sovereign God,

I will praise Your name for ever.

Every day I will praise You;

I will extol Your name for ever.

גָּדוֹל יהוה וּמְהֻלָּל מְאֹד, וְלִגְדֻלָּתוֹ אֵין חֵקֶר.

דּוֹר לְדוֹר יְשַׁבַּח מַעֲשֶׂיךָ, וּגְבוּרֹתֶיךָ יַגִּידוּ.

Great are You, Eternal One, and worthy of praise;

and infinite is Your greatness.

Several verses of this psalm are translated into second person,
to maintain gender-neutrality in the English text.

One generation shall acclaim Your work to the next;
they shall tell of Your mighty acts.

הֲדַר כְּבוֹד הוֹדֶךָ, וְדִבְרֵי נִפְלְאֹתֶיךָ אָשִׂיחָה.
וֶעֱזוּז נוֹרְאֹתֶיךָ יֹאמֵרוּ, וּגְדֻלָּתְךָ אֲסַפְּרֶנָּה.

They shall bring word of Your radiant glory;
and bear witness to Your wondrous works.

They shall speak of Your awesome might,
and make known Your greatness.

זֵכֶר רַב־טוּבְךָ יַבִּיעוּ, וְצִדְקָתְךָ יְרַנֵּנוּ.
חַנּוּן וְרַחוּם יהוה, אֶרֶךְ אַפַּיִם וּגְדָל־חָסֶד.
טוֹב־יהוה לַכֹּל, וְרַחֲמָיו עַל־כָּל־מַעֲשָׂיו.

They shall tell the world of Your goodness,
and sing of Your righteousness.

"God is gracious and compassionate,
endlessly patient, overflowing with love."
*"You are good to all; Your compassion
shelters all Your creatures."*

יוֹדוּךָ יהוה כָּל מַעֲשֶׂיךָ, וַחֲסִידֶיךָ יְבָרְכוּכָה.
כְּבוֹד מַלְכוּתְךָ יֹאמֵרוּ, וּגְבוּרָתְךָ יְדַבֵּרוּ.

All Your works shall glorify You;
Your faithful ones shall praise You.

They shall proclaim Your majestic glory,
they shall tell of Your might:

לְהוֹדִיעַ לִבְנֵי הָאָדָם גְּבוּרֹתָיו, וּכְבוֹד הֲדַר מַלְכוּתוֹ.
מַלְכוּתְךָ מַלְכוּת כָּל־עֹלָמִים, וּמֶמְשַׁלְתְּךָ בְּכָל־דּוֹר וָדֹר.

To reveal Your power to the world,

and the glorious splendor of Your rule.

You are sovereign to the end of time;

You reign through all generations.

סוֹמֵךְ יהוה לְכָל־הַנֹּפְלִים, וְזוֹקֵף לְכָל־הַכְּפוּפִים.

עֵינֵי־כֹל אֵלֶיךָ יְשַׂבֵּרוּ, וְאַתָּה נוֹתֵן־לָהֶם אֶת־אָכְלָם בְּעִתּוֹ.

You support the falling, Eternal One;

You raise up all who are bowed down.

The eyes of all are turned to You;

You sustain them in time of need.

פּוֹתֵחַ אֶת־יָדֶךָ וּמַשְׂבִּיעַ לְכָל־חַי רָצוֹן.

צַדִּיק יהוה בְּכָל־דְּרָכָיו, וְחָסִיד בְּכָל־מַעֲשָׂיו.

You open Your hand,

to fulfill the needs of all the living.

You are just in all Your ways,

loving in all Your deeds.

קָרוֹב יהוה לְכָל־קֹרְאָיו, לְכֹל אֲשֶׁר יִקְרָאֻהוּ בֶאֱמֶת.

רְצוֹן־יְרֵאָיו יַעֲשֶׂה, וְאֶת־שַׁוְעָתָם יִשְׁמַע וְיוֹשִׁיעֵם.

שׁוֹמֵר יהוה אֶת־כָּל־אֹהֲבָיו, וְאֵת כָּל־הָרְשָׁעִים יַשְׁמִיד.

You are near to all who call upon You,

to all who call upon You in truth.

You fulfill the hope of all who revere You;

You hear their cry and help them.

תְּהִלַּת יהוה יְדַבֶּר־פִּי

וִיבָרֵךְ כָּל־בָּשָׂר שֵׁם קָדְשׁוֹ לְעוֹלָם וָעֶד.

וַאֲנַחְנוּ נְבָרֵךְ יָהּ מֵעַתָּה וְעַד־עוֹלָם. הַלְלוּיָהּ.

My lips shall declare the glory of God;
let all flesh praise Your holy name for ever and ever.

We will praise Your name now and always. Halleluyah!

All rise

READER'S KADDISH   חצי קדיש

יִתְגַּדַּל וְיִתְקַדַּשׁ שְׁמֵהּ רַבָּא בְּעָלְמָא דִי־בְרָא כִרְעוּתֵהּ,
וְיַמְלִיךְ מַלְכוּתֵהּ בְּחַיֵּיכוֹן וּבְיוֹמֵיכוֹן וּבְחַיֵּי דְכָל־בֵּית
יִשְׂרָאֵל, בַּעֲגָלָא וּבִזְמַן קָרִיב, וְאִמְרוּ: אָמֵן.

יְהֵא שְׁמֵהּ רַבָּא מְבָרַךְ לְעָלַם וּלְעָלְמֵי עָלְמַיָּא.

יִתְבָּרַךְ וְיִשְׁתַּבַּח, וְיִתְפָּאַר וְיִתְרוֹמַם וְיִתְנַשֵּׂא, וְיִתְהַדָּר
וְיִתְעַלֶּה וְיִתְהַלָּל שְׁמֵהּ דְּקוּדְשָׁא, בְּרִיךְ הוּא, לְעֵלָּא
מִן־כָּל־בִּרְכָתָא וְשִׁירָתָא, תֻּשְׁבְּחָתָא וְנֶחֱמָתָא דַּאֲמִירָן
בְּעָלְמָא, וְאִמְרוּ: אָמֵן.

Yit-ga-dal v'yit-ka-dash sh'mei ra-ba b'al-ma di-v'ra chir-u-tei,
v'yam-lich mal-chu-tei b'cha-yei-chon u-v'yo-mei-chon u-v'cha-yei
d'chol beit Yis-ra-eil, ba-a-ga-la u-viz-man ka-riv, v'im'ru: A-mein.

Y'hei sh'mei ra-ba m'va-rach l'a-lam u-l'al-mei al-ma-ya.

Yit-ba-rach v'yish-ta-bach v'yit-pa-ar, v'yit-ro-mam, v'yit-na-sei, v'yit-
ha-dar, v'yit-a-leh, v'yit-ha-lal sh'mei d'kud'sha, b'rich hu, l'ei-la min
kol bir-cha-ta v'shi-ra-ta, tush-b'cha-ta v'neh-cheh-ma-ta da-a-mi-
ran b'al-ma, v'im'ru: A-mein.

Let the glory of God be extolled, and God's great name be hallowed in the world whose creation God willed. May God rule in our own day, in our own lives, and in the life of all Israel, and let us say: Amen.

Let God's great name be blessed for ever and ever.

Beyond all the praises, songs, and adorations that we can utter is the Holy One, the Blessed One, whom yet we glorify, honor, and exalt. And let us say: Amen.

Alternative forms of the T'filah are on pages 31, 45, 57

Torah Service   סדר קריאת התורה

אֵין כָּמוֹךָ בָאֱלֹהִים, יי, וְאֵין כְּמַעֲשֶׂיךָ.
מַלְכוּתְךָ מַלְכוּת כָּל־עוֹלָמִים וּמֶמְשַׁלְתְּךָ בְּכָל־דּוֹר וָדֹר.

יי מֶלֶךְ, יי מָלָךְ, יי יִמְלֹךְ לְעוֹלָם וָעֶד.
יהוה עֹז לְעַמּוֹ יִתֵּן, יהוה יְבָרֵךְ אֶת־עַמּוֹ בַשָּׁלוֹם.

Adonai me-lech, Adonai ma-lach, Adonai yim-loch l'-olam va-ed.
Adonai oz l'-a-mo yi-tein, Adonai y'-va-reich et a-mo va-sha-lom.

There is none like You, Eternal One, among the gods that are
worshipped, and there are no deeds like Yours. Your sovereignty
is everlasting; You reign through all generations.

God rules; God will reign for ever and ever.
Eternal God, give strength to Your people;
Eternal God, bless Your people with peace.

All rise

אֵל הָרַחֲמִים, הֵיטִיבָה בִרְצוֹנְךָ אֶת־צִיּוֹן;
תִּבְנֶה חוֹמוֹת יְרוּשָׁלָיִם.
כִּי בְךָ לְבַד בָּטָחְנוּ, מֶלֶךְ אֵל רָם וְנִשָּׂא, אֲדוֹן עוֹלָמִים.

Eil ha-ra-cha-mim hei-ti-va vir'tso-n'cha et tsi-yon, tiv-nei cho-mot
Y'ru-sha-la-yim.
Ki v'cha l'vad ba-tach-nu me-lech, Eil ram v'ni-sa, A-don o-la-mim.

Source of mercy, let Your goodness be a blessing to Zion; let
Jerusalem be rebuilt. In You alone do we trust, O Sovereign
God, high and exalted, Ruler of all the worlds.

THE ARK IS OPENED

הָבוּ גֹֽדֶל לֵאלֹהֵֽינוּ וּתְנוּ כָבוֹד לַתּוֹרָה.

Let us declare the greatness of our God and give honor to the Torah.

THE TORAH IS TAKEN FROM THE ARK

כִּי מִצִּיּוֹן תֵּצֵא תוֹרָה, וּדְבַר־יהוה מִירוּשָׁלָֽיִם.

בָּרוּךְ שֶׁנָּתַן תּוֹרָה לְעַמּוֹ יִשְׂרָאֵל בִּקְדֻשָּׁתוֹ.

Ki mi-tsi-yon tei-tsei Torah, u-d'-var Adonai mi-ru-sha-la-yim.

Ba-ruch she-na-tan Torah l'-amo Yis-ra-eil bi-k'du-sha-to.

For out of Zion shall go forth Torah, and the word of God from Jerusalem. Praised be the One who in holiness gives Torah to our people Israel.

בֵּית יַעֲקֹב, לְכוּ וְנֵלְכָה בְּאוֹר יהוה:

O House of Israel, let us walk by the light of our God.

❖ ❖

שְׁמַע יִשְׂרָאֵל: יהוה אֱלֹהֵֽינוּ, יהוה אֶחָד!

Sh'ma Yis-ra-eil: Adonai Eh-lo-hei-nu, Adonai Eh-chad!

Hear, O Israel: the Eternal One is our God,
the Eternal God alone!

אֶחָד אֱלֹהֵֽינוּ, גָּדוֹל אֲדוֹנֵֽינוּ, קָדוֹשׁ שְׁמוֹ.

Eh-chad Eh-lo-hei-nu, ga-dol A-doh-nei-nu, ka-dosh sh'mo.

Our God is One; great and holy is the Eternal One.

❖ ❖

גַּדְּלוּ לַיהוה אִתִּי וּנְרוֹמְמָה שְׁמוֹ יַחְדָּו.

O magnify the Eternal One with me, and together let us exalt
God's name.

לְךָ, יהוה, הַגְּדֻלָּה וְהַגְּבוּרָה וְהַתִּפְאֶרֶת וְהַנֵּצַח וְהַהוֹד, כִּי
כֹל בַּשָּׁמַיִם וּבָאָרֶץ, לְךָ יהוה הַמַּמְלָכָה וְהַמִּתְנַשֵּׂא
לְכֹל לְרֹאשׁ.

L'cha Adonai ha-g'du-lah v'ha-g'vu-rah v'ha-tif-e-ret v'ha-nei-tzach
v'ha-hod, ki chol ba-sha-ma-yim u-va-a-retz. L'cha Adonai ha-
mam-la-cha, v'ha-mit-na-sei l'chol l'rosh.

Yours, O God, is the greatness, the power, the glory, the victory,
and the majesty, for all that is in heaven and earth is Yours. You,
O God, are sovereign; You are supreme over all.

All are seated

Reading of the Torah

BEFORE THE READING

בָּרְכוּ אֶת־יי הַמְבֹרָךְ!

בָּרוּךְ יי הַמְבֹרָךְ לְעוֹלָם וָעֶד!

בָּרוּךְ יי הַמְבֹרָךְ לְעוֹלָם וָעֶד!

בָּרוּךְ אַתָּה יי, אֱלֹהֵינוּ מֶלֶךְ הָעוֹלָם, אֲשֶׁר

בָּחַר־בָּנוּ מִכָּל־הָעַמִּים וְנָתַן־לָנוּ אֶת־תּוֹרָתוֹ.

בָּרוּךְ אַתָּה יי, נוֹתֵן הַתּוֹרָה.

READER: Ba-r'chu et Adonai ha-m'vo-rach!

CONGREGATION: Ba-ruch Adonai ha-m'vo-rach l'o-lam va-ed!

READER: Ba-ruch Adonai ha-m'vo-rach l'o-lam va-ed!

Ba-ruch a-ta Adonai, Eh-lo-hei-nu meh-lech ha-o-lam, a-sher ba-
char ba-nu mi-kol ha-a-mim, v'na-tan la-nu et Torah-toh. Ba-ruch
a-ta A-donai, no-tein ha-Torah.

Praise the One, to whom our praise is due!

Praised be the One to whom our praise is due,
now and for ever!

Praised be the One to whom our praise is due, now and for ever!

We praise You, Eternal God of time and space: You have chosen us from all peoples by giving us the Torah. We praise You, Eternal One, Giver of the Torah.

AFTER THE READING

בָּרוּךְ אַתָּה יי, אֱלֹהֵינוּ מֶלֶךְ הָעוֹלָם, אֲשֶׁר נָתַן לָנוּ
תּוֹרַת אֱמֶת וְחַיֵּי עוֹלָם נָטַע בְּתוֹכֵנוּ. בָּרוּךְ אַתָּה יי,
נוֹתֵן הַתּוֹרָה.

Ba-ruch a-ta Adonai, Eh-lo-hei-nu meh-lech ha-o-lam, a-sher na-tan la-nu Toh-rat eh-met, v'cha-yei o-lam na-ta b'toh-chei-nu. Ba-ruch a-ta Adonai, no-tein ha-Torah.

We praise You, Eternal God of time and space: You have given us a Torah of truth, implanting within us eternal life. We praise You, Eternal One, Giver of the Torah.

(As the reading is completed, the Torah might be held high,
while this is said or sung)

וְזֹאת הַתּוֹרָה אֲשֶׁר־שָׂם מֹשֶׁה לִפְנֵי בְּנֵי יִשְׂרָאֵל, עַל־פִּי יי
בְּיַד־מֹשֶׁה.

V'zot ha-to-rah a-sher sam Mo-sheh lif-nei b'nei Yis-ra-eil al pi Adonai b'yad Mo-sheh.

This is the Torah that Moses placed before the people of Israel.

71

Returning the Torah to the Ark

All rise

יְהַלְלוּ אֶת־שֵׁם יהוה, כִּי נִשְׂגָּב שְׁמוֹ לְבַדּוֹ.

Y'-ha-l'lu et sheim Adonai, ki nis-gav sh'mo l'va-do.

Let us praise the Eternal God, whose name alone is exalted.

הוֹדוֹ עַל אֶרֶץ וְשָׁמָיִם, וַיָּרֶם קֶרֶן לְעַמּוֹ, תְּהִלָּה
לְכָל־חֲסִידָיו, לִבְנֵי יִשְׂרָאֵל עַם קְרוֹבוֹ. הַלְלוּיָהּ!

Ho-do al e-retz v'sha-ma-yim, va-ya-rem ke-ren l'a-mo, t'hi-la l'chol
cha-si-dav li-v'nei Yis-ra-eil am k'ro-vo, Ha-l'lu-yah!

Your splendor covers heaven and earth; You are the strength of Your
people, making glorious Your faithful ones, Israel, a people close to
You. Halleluyah!

❖ ❖

תּוֹרַת יהוה תְּמִימָה, מְשִׁיבַת נָפֶשׁ;
עֵדוּת יהוה נֶאֱמָנָה, מַחְכִּימַת פֶּתִי.

God's Torah is perfect, reviving the soul;

God's teaching is sure, making wise the simple.

פִּקּוּדֵי יהוה יְשָׁרִים, מְשַׂמְּחֵי־לֵב;
מִצְוַת יהוה בָּרָה, מְאִירַת עֵינָיִם.

God's precepts are right, delighting the mind;

God's Mitzvah is clear, giving light to the eyes.

יִרְאַת יהוה טְהוֹרָה, עֹמֶדֶת לָעַד;
מִשְׁפְּטֵי יהוה אֱמֶת, צָדְקוּ יַחְדָּו.

God's word is pure, enduring for ever;

God's judgments are true, and altogether just.

❖ ❖

Behold, a good doctrine has been given you, My Torah; do not forsake it. It is a tree of life to those who hold it fast, and all who cling to it find happiness. Its ways are ways of pleasantness, and all its paths are peace.

כִּי לֶקַח טוֹב נָתַתִּי לָכֶם, תּוֹרָתִי אַל־תַּעֲזֹבוּ.

Ki le-kach tov na-ta-ti la-chem, to-ra-ti al ta-a-zo-vu.

עֵץ־חַיִּים הִיא לַמַּחֲזִיקִים בָּהּ, וְתֹמְכֶיהָ מְאֻשָּׁר.
דְּרָכֶיהָ דַרְכֵי־נֹעַם, וְכָל־נְתִיבוֹתֶיהָ שָׁלוֹם.

Eitz cha-yim hi la-ma-cha-zi-kim bah, v'to-m'che-ha m'u-shar.
D'ra-che-ha dar-chei no-am v'chol n'ti-vo-te-ha sha-lom.

Help us to return to You, O God; then truly shall we return. Renew our days as in the past.

הֲשִׁיבֵנוּ יהוה אֵלֶיךָ, וְנָשׁוּבָה. חַדֵּשׁ יָמֵינוּ כְּקֶדֶם.

Ha-shi-vei-nu Adonai ei-le-cha, v'na-shu-va. Cha-deish ya-mei-nu k'ke-dem.

THE ARK IS CLOSED

All are seated

Service at a House of Mourning begins on page 88

73

Aleinu I

עָלֵינוּ

All rise

עָלֵינוּ לְשַׁבֵּחַ לַאֲדוֹן הַכֹּל, לָתֵת גְּדֻלָּה לְיוֹצֵר בְּרֵאשִׁית,
שֶׁלֹּא עָשָׂנוּ כְּגוֹיֵי הָאֲרָצוֹת, וְלֹא שָׂמָנוּ כְּמִשְׁפְּחוֹת
הָאֲדָמָה; שֶׁלֹּא שָׂם חֶלְקֵנוּ כָּהֶם, וְגוֹרָלֵנוּ כְּכָל־הֲמוֹנָם.

וַאֲנַחְנוּ כּוֹרְעִים וּמִשְׁתַּחֲוִים וּמוֹדִים לִפְנֵי
מֶלֶךְ מַלְכֵי הַמְּלָכִים, הַקָּדוֹשׁ בָּרוּךְ הוּא.

A-lei-nu l'sha-bei-ach la-a-don ha-kol, la-teit g'du-la l'yo-tzeir b'rei-
shit, sheh-lo a-sa-nu k'go-yei ha-a-ra-tzot, v'lo sa-ma-nu k'mish-
p'choht ha-a-da-ma; sheh-lo sam chel-kei-nu ka-hem, v'go-ra-lei-nu
k'chol ha-mo-nam.

Va-a-nach-nu ko-r'im u-mish-ta-cha-vim u-mo-dim lif-nei meh-lech
mal-chei ha-m'la-chim, ha-ka-dosh ba-ruch hu.

We must praise the God of all, the Maker of heaven and earth, who
has set us apart from the other families of earth, giving us a destiny
unique among the nations.

Therefore we bow in awe and thanksgiving before the One who is
sovereign over all, the Holy and Blessed One.

שֶׁהוּא נוֹטֶה שָׁמַיִם וְיוֹסֵד אָרֶץ, וּמוֹשַׁב יְקָרוֹ בַּשָּׁמַיִם מִמַּעַל
וּשְׁכִינַת עֻזּוֹ בְּגָבְהֵי מְרוֹמִים. הוּא אֱלֹהֵינוּ, אֵין עוֹד;
אֱמֶת מַלְכֵּנוּ, אֶפֶס זוּלָתוֹ, כַּכָּתוּב בְּתוֹרָתוֹ: "וְיָדַעְתָּ הַיּוֹם
וַהֲשֵׁבֹתָ אֶל־לְבָבֶךָ, כִּי יי הוּא הָאֱלֹהִים בַּשָּׁמַיִם מִמַּעַל
וְעַל־הָאָרֶץ מִתָּחַת, אֵין עוֹד."

She-hu no-teh sha-ma-yim v'yo-seid a-retz u-mo-shav y'ka-ro ba-
sha-ma-yim mi-ma-al ush'chi-nat u-zo b'gov-hei m'ro-mim. Hu Eh-
lo-hei-nu ein od; eh-met mal-kei-nu eh-fes zu-la-to ka-ka-tuv b'toh-
ra-to. V'ya-da-ta ha-yom v'ha-sheh-vo-ta el l'va-ve-cha, ki A-do-nai
hu ha-eh-lo-him ba-sha-ma-yim mi-ma-al v'al ha-a-retz mi-ta-chat,
ein od.

You spread out the heavens and established the earth; You are
our God; there is none else. In truth You alone are our sovereign
God, as it is written: "Know then this day and take it to heart:
the Eternal One is God in the heavens above and on the earth
below; there is none else."

עַל־כֵּן נְקַוֶּה לְךָ, יי אֱלֹהֵינוּ, לִרְאוֹת מְהֵרָה בְּתִפְאֶרֶת
עֻזֶּךָ, לְהַעֲבִיר גִּלּוּלִים מִן הָאָרֶץ, וְהָאֱלִילִים כָּרוֹת יִכָּרֵתוּן,
לְתַקֵּן עוֹלָם בְּמַלְכוּת שַׁדַּי, וְכָל־בְּנֵי בָשָׂר יִקְרְאוּ בִשְׁמֶךָ,
לְהַפְנוֹת אֵלֶיךָ כָּל־רִשְׁעֵי אָרֶץ.

We therefore hope, our Eternal God, soon to behold the
glory of Your might. Then will false gods vanish from our
hearts, and the world be perfected under Your unchal-
lenged rule. And then will all acclaim You as their God,
and, forsaking evil, turn to You alone.

יַכִּירוּ וְיֵדְעוּ כָּל־יוֹשְׁבֵי תֵבֵל כִּי לְךָ תִּכְרַע כָּל־בֶּרֶךְ,
תִּשָּׁבַע כָּל־לָשׁוֹן. לְפָנֶיךָ, יי אֱלֹהֵינוּ, יִכְרְעוּ וְיִפֹּלוּ,
וְלִכְבוֹד שִׁמְךָ יְקָר יִתֵּנוּ, וִיקַבְּלוּ כֻלָּם אֶת־עֹל מַלְכוּתֶךָ,
וְתִמְלֹךְ עֲלֵיהֶם מְהֵרָה לְעוֹלָם וָעֶד.

Let all who dwell on earth acknowledge that unto You ev-
ery knee must bend and every tongue swear loyalty. Before
You, let them humble themselves. To Your glorious name let
them give honor. Let all accept You as their Ruler, that You
may reign over them soon and for ever.

כִּי הַמַּלְכוּת שֶׁלְּךָ הִיא, וּלְעוֹלְמֵי עַד תִּמְלוֹךְ בְּכָבוֹד.
כַּכָּתוּב בְּתוֹרָתֶךָ: "יהוה יִמְלֹךְ לְעֹלָם וָעֶד."

*For You are sovereign, and to all eternity You will reign in
glory, as it is written: "God will reign for ever and ever."*

וְנֶאֱמַר: "וְהָיָה יהוה לְמֶלֶךְ עַל־כָּל־הָאָרֶץ;
בַּיּוֹם הַהוּא יִהְיֶה יהוה אֶחָד וּשְׁמוֹ אֶחָד."

V'neh-eh-mar: V'ha-yah Adonai l'meh-lech al kol ha-a-retz; ba-yom
ha-hu yi-h'yeh Adonai Eh-chad, u-sh'mo Eh-chad.

And it has been said: "The Eternal God shall rule over all the earth;
On that day You shall be One and Your name shall be One."

Continue on page 79

Aleinu II

עֲלֵינוּ

All rise

עָלֵינוּ לְשַׁבֵּחַ לַאֲדוֹן הַכֹּל, לָתֵת גְּדֻלָּה לְיוֹצֵר בְּרֵאשִׁית,
שֶׁהוּא שָׂם חֶלְקֵנוּ לְיַחֵד אֶת־שְׁמוֹ, וְגוֹרָלֵנוּ לְהַמְלִיךְ מַלְכוּתוֹ.

A-lei-nu l'sha-bei-ach la-a-don ha-kol, la-teit g'du-la l'yo-tzeir b'rei-
shit, she-hu sahm chei-kei-nu l'ya-cheid et sh'mo, v'go-ra-lei-nu
l'ham-lich mal-chu-toh.

°*Let us adore the ever-living God! We render praise unto You who
spread out the heavens and establish the earth, whose glory is
revealed in the heavens above, and whose greatness is manifest
throughout the world. You are our God; there is none else.*

וַאֲנַחְנוּ כּוֹרְעִים וּמִשְׁתַּחֲוִים וּמוֹדִים לִפְנֵי
מֶלֶךְ מַלְכֵי הַמְּלָכִים, הַקָּדוֹשׁ בָּרוּךְ הוּא.

Va-a-nach-nu ko-r'im u-mish-ta-cha-vim u-mo-dim lif-nei meh-lech
mal-chei ha-m'la-chim, ha-ka-dosh ba-ruch hu.

Therefore we bow in awe and thanksgiving before the One who is
sovereign over all, the Holy and Blessed One.

All are seated

May the time not be distant, O God, when Your name shall be
worshipped in all the earth, when unbelief shall disappear and
error be no more. Fervently we pray that the day may come
when all shall turn to You in love, when corruption and evil
shall give way to integrity and goodness, when superstition shall
no longer enslave the mind, nor idolatry blind the eye, when all
who dwell on earth shall know that You alone are God. O may
all, created in Your image, become one in spirit and one in

friendship, for ever united in Your service. Then shall Your rule be established on earth, and the word of Your prophet fulfilled: "The Eternal God will reign for ever and ever."

On that day, O God, You shall be One
and Your name shall be One.

בַּיּוֹם הַהוּא יִהְיֶה יהוה אֶחָד וּשְׁמוֹ אֶחָד.

Ba-yom ha-hu yi-h'yeh Adonai Eh-chad, u-sh'mo Eh-chad.

Before the Kaddish

Our thoughts turn to those who have departed this earth: our own loved ones, those whom our friends and neighbors have lost, the martyrs of our people, and those of every race and nation whose lives have been a blessing to humanity. As we remember them, let us meditate on the meaning of love and loss, of life and death.

❖ ❖

MEDITATIONS

❧ 1. THE TRADITION OF THE KADDISH

The origins of the Kaddish are mysterious; angels are said to have brought it down from heaven. . . .

It possesses wonderful power. Truly, if there is any bond strong enough to chain heaven to earth, it is this prayer. It keeps the living together, and forms a bridge to the mysterious realm of the dead. One might almost say that this prayer is the . . . guardian of the people by whom alone it is uttered; therein lies the warrant of its continuance. Can a people disappear and be annihilated so long as a child remembers its parents?

Because this prayer does not acknowledge death, because it permits the blossom, which has fallen from the tree of humankind, to flower and develop again in the human heart, therefore it possesses sanctifying power.

❧ 2. FACING DEATH

The contemplation of death should plant within the soul elevation and peace. Above all, it should make us see things in their true light. For all things which seem foolish in the light of death are really foolish in themselves. To be annoyed because So-and-so has slighted us or has been somewhat more successful in social distinctions, pulled himself somehow one rung higher up the ladder than ourselves—how ridiculous all this seems when we couple it with the thought of death!

To pass each day simply and solely in the eager pursuit of money or fame, this also seems like living with shadows when one might take one's part with realities. Surely when death is at hand we should desire to say, 'I have contributed my grain to the great store of the eternal. I have borne my part in the struggle for goodness.' And let no man or woman suppose that the smallest social act of goodness is wasted for society at large. All our help, petty though it be, is needed; and though we know not the manner, the fruit of every faithful service is gathered in. Let the true and noble words of a great teacher ring in conclusion upon our ears: 'The growing good of the world is partly dependent on unhistoric acts; and that things are not so ill with you and me as they might have been, is half owing to the number who lived faithfully a hidden life and rest in unvisited tombs.'

❧ 3. IN RECENT GRIEF

When cherished ties are broken, and the chain of love is shattered, only trust and the strength of faith can lighten the heaviness of the heart. At times, the pain of separation seems more than we can bear; but love and understanding can help us pass through the darkness toward the light.

Out of affliction the Psalmist learned the law of God. And in truth, grief is a great teacher, when it sends us back to serve and bless the living. We learn how to counsel and comfort those who, like ourselves, are bowed with sorrow. We learn when to keep silence in their presence, and when a word will assure them of our love and concern.

Thus, even when they are gone, the departed are with us, moving us to live as, in their higher moments, they themselves wished to live. We remember them now; they live in our hearts; they are an abiding blessing.

❧ 4. AFTER A TRAGIC LOSS

O God, help me to live with my grief!

Death has taken my beloved, and I feel that I cannot go on. My faith is shaken; my mind keeps asking: Why? Why does joy end in sorrow? Why does love exact its price in tears? Why?

O God, help me to live with my grief!

Help me to accept the mystery of life. Help me to see that even if my questions were answered, even if I did know why, the pain would be no less, the loneliness would remain bitter beyond words. Still my heart would ache.

O God, help me to triumph over my grief!

Help me to endure this night of anguish. Help me to walk through the darkness with faith in tomorrow. Give me comfort; give me courage; turn me to deeds that bless the living.

O God, help me to triumph over my grief.

❧ 5. HOW CAN WE UNDERSTAND DEATH?

What can we know of death, we who cannot understand life?

We study the seed and the cell, but the power deep within them will always elude us.

Though we cannot understand, we accept life as the gift of God. Yet death, life's twin, we face with fear.

But why be afraid? Death is a haven to the weary, a relief for the sorely afflicted. We are safe in death as in life.

There is no pain in death. There is only the pain of the living as they recall shared loves, and as they themselves fear to die.

Calm us, O God, when we cry out in our fear and our grief. Turn us anew toward life and the world. Awaken us to the warmth of human love that speaks to us of You.

We shall fear no evil, for You are with us.

❧ 6. A PHILOSOPHY OF LIFE AND DEATH

Judaism teaches us to understand death as part of the Divine pattern of the universe. Actually, we could not have our sensitivity without fragility. Mortality is the tax that we pay for the privilege of love, thought, creative work—the toll on the bridge of being from which clods of earth and snow-peaked mountain summits are exempt. Just because we are human, we are prisoners of the years. Yet that very prison is the room of discipline in which we, driven by the urgency of time, create.

❧ 7. THE BLESSING OF MEMORY

It is hard to sing of oneness when our world is not complete, when those who once brought wholeness to our life have gone, and naught but memory can fill the emptiness their passing leaves behind.

But memory can tell us only what we were, in company with those we loved; it cannot help us find what each of us, alone, must now become. Yet no one is really alone; those who live no more, echo still within our thoughts and words, and what they did is part of what we have become.

We do best homage to our dead when we live our lives most fully, even in the shadow of our loss. For each of our lives is worth the life of the whole world; in each one is the breath of the Ultimate One. In affirming the One, we affirm the worth of each one whose life, now ended, brought us closer to the Source of life, in whose unity no one is alone and every life finds purpose.

8. IN PRAISE OF LIVES NOW GONE

. . . יִתְגַּדַּל וְיִתְקַדַּשׁ שְׁמֵהּ רַבָּא

This the profound praise of the living,
Praise for the generous gift of life.
Praise for the presence of loved ones,
    the bonds of friendship,
    the link of memory.

Praise for the toil and searching,
    the dedication and vision,
    the ennobling aspirations.

Praise for the precious moorings of faith,
    for courageous souls,
    for prophets, psalmists, and sages.

Praise for those who walked before us,
    the sufferers in the valley of shadows,
    the steadfast in the furnace of hate.

. . . יִתְגַּדַּל וְיִתְקַדַּשׁ שְׁמֵהּ רַבָּא

Praise for the God of our people,
    the Source of all growth and goodness.
    the Promise on which we build tomorrow.

9. WE LIVE IN OUR WORK

Everlasting God, the generations come and go before You. Brief is their time. Passing, they leave many of their tasks unfinished, their plans unfulfilled, their dreams unrealized. It would be more than we could bear, but for the faith that our little day finds its permanence in Your eternity, and our work its completion in the unfolding of Your purpose for humanity.

At this sacred moment we turn our thoughts to those who have gone from life. We recall the joy of their companionship. We feel a pang, the echo of that intenser grief when first their death lay before our stricken eyes. Now we know that they will never vanish, so long as heart and thought remain within us. By love are they remembered, and in memory they live.

Creator of life, grant that the memory of our loved ones may bring strength and blessing. May the goodness of their lives and the high ideals they cherished endure in our thoughts and live on in our deeds. Amen

❧ 10. THE LIFE OF ETERNITY

The light of life is finite. It is kindled, it burns, it glows, it is radiant with warmth and beauty. But soon it fades; its substance is consumed, and it is no more.

In light we see; in light we are seen. The flames dance and our lives are full. But as night follows day, the candle of our life burns down and gutters. There is an end to the flames. We see no more and are no more seen. Yet we do not despair, for we are more than a memory slowly fading into the darkness. With our lives we give life. Something of us can never die: we move in the eternal cycle of darkness and death, of light and life.

❧ 11. THE SPIRIT LIVES ON

"God gives; God takes away; blessed be the name of God."

Early or late, all must answer the summons to return to the Reservoir of Being. For we loose our hold on life when our time has come, as the leaf falls from the bough when its day is done. The deeds of the righteous enrich the world, as the fallen leaf enriches the soil beneath. The dust returns to the earth, the spirit lives on with God.

Like the stars by day, our beloved dead are not seen by mortal eyes. Yet they shine on for ever; theirs is eternal peace.

Let us be thankful for the companionship that continues in a love stronger than death. Sanctifying the name of God, we do honor to their memory.

❧ 12. STRENGTH FOR THOSE WHO MOURN

In nature's ebb and flow, Your eternal law abides. As You are our support in the struggles of life, so, also, are You our hope in death. In Your care, O God, are the souls of all the living and the spirits of all flesh. Your power gives us strength; Your love comforts us. O Life of our life, Soul of our soul, cause Your light to shine into our hearts. Fill us with trust in You, and turn us again to the tasks of life. And may the memory of our loved ones inspire us to continue their work for the coming of Your sovereign rule.

❧ 13. OUR MARTYRS

We have lived in numberless towns and villages; and in too many of them we have endured cruel suffering. Some we have forgotten; others are sealed into our memory, a wound that does not heal. A hundred generations of victims and martyrs; still their blood cries out from the earth. And so many, so many at Dachau, at Buchenwald, at Babi Yar, and . . . .

What can we say? What can we do? How bear the unbearable, or accept what life has brought to our people? All who are born must die, but how shall we compare the slow passage of our days with the callous slaughter of the innocent, cut off before their time?

They lived with faith. Not all, but many. And, surely, many died with faith; faith in God, in life, in the goodness that even flames cannot destroy. May we find a way to the strength of that faith, that trust, that sure sense that life and soul endure beyond this body's death.

They have left their lives to us: let a million prayers rise whenever Jews worship; let a million candles glow against the darkness of these unfinished lives.

❖ ❖

We recall the loved ones whom death has recently taken from us . . . . And we remember those who died at this season in years past, whom we have taken into our hearts with our own . . . . The memories of all of them are with us; our griefs and sympathies are mingled. Loving God, we praise Your name:

Mourner's Kaddish קדיש יתום

יִתְגַּדַּל וְיִתְקַדַּשׁ שְׁמֵהּ רַבָּא בְּעָלְמָא דִי־בְרָא כִרְעוּתֵהּ, וְיַמְלִיךְ מַלְכוּתֵהּ בְּחַיֵּיכוֹן וּבְיוֹמֵיכוֹן וּבְחַיֵּי דְכָל־בֵּית יִשְׂרָאֵל, בַּעֲגָלָא וּבִזְמַן קָרִיב, וְאִמְרוּ: אָמֵן.

Yit-ga-dal v'yit-ka-dash sh'mei ra-ba b'al-ma di-v'ra chir-u-tei,
v'yam-lich mal-chu-tei b'cha-yei-chon u-v'yo-mei-chon u-v'cha-yei
d'chol beit Yis-ra-eil, ba-a-ga-la u-viz-man ka-riv, v'im-ru: A-mein.

יְהֵא שְׁמֵהּ רַבָּא מְבָרַךְ לְעָלַם וּלְעָלְמֵי עָלְמַיָּא.

Y'hei sh'mei ra-ba m'va-rach l'a-lam u-l'al-mei al-ma-ya.

יִתְבָּרַךְ וְיִשְׁתַּבַּח, וְיִתְפָּאַר וְיִתְרוֹמַם וְיִתְנַשֵּׂא, וְיִתְהַדָּר וְיִתְעַלֶּה וְיִתְהַלָּל שְׁמֵהּ דְּקוּדְשָׁא, בְּרִיךְ הוּא,

Yit-ba-rach v'yish-ta-bach v'yit-pa-ar, v'yit-ro-mam, v'yit-na-sei,
v'yit-ha-dar, v'yit-a-leh, v'yit-ha-lal sh'mei d'kud'sha, b'rich hu,

לְעֵלָּא מִן־כָּל־בִּרְכָתָא וְשִׁירָתָא, תֻּשְׁבְּחָתָא וְנֶחֱמָתָא דַּאֲמִירָן בְּעָלְמָא, וְאִמְרוּ: אָמֵן.

L'ei-la min kol bir-cha-ta v'shi-ra-ta, tush-b'cha-ta v'neh-cheh-ma-ta
da-a-mi-ran b'al-ma, v'im-ru: A-mein.

יְהֵא שְׁלָמָא רַבָּא מִן־שְׁמַיָּא וְחַיִּים עָלֵינוּ וְעַל־כָּל־
יִשְׂרָאֵל, וְאִמְרוּ: אָמֵן.

Y'hei sh'la-ma ra-ba min sh'ma-ya v'cha-yim, a-lei-nu v'al kol
Yis-ra-eil, v'im-ru: A-mein.

עֹשֶׂה שָׁלוֹם בִּמְרוֹמָיו, הוּא יַעֲשֶׂה שָׁלוֹם עָלֵינוּ וְעַל־כָּל־
יִשְׂרָאֵל, וְאִמְרוּ: אָמֵן.

O-seh sha-lom bim-ro-mav, hu ya-a-seh sha-lom a-lei-nu v'al kol
Yis-ra-eil, v'im-ru: A-mein.

Let the glory of God be extolled, and God's great name be hallowed in the
world whose creation God willed. May God rule in our own day, in our
own lives, and in the life of all Israel, and let us say: Amen.

Let God's great name be blessed for ever and ever.

Beyond all the praises, songs, and adorations that we can utter is the Holy
One, the Blessed One, whom yet we glorify, honor, and exalt. And let us
say: Amen.

For us and for all Israel, may the blessing of peace and the promise of life
come true, and let us say: Amen.

May the One who causes peace to reign in the high heavens, let peace
descend on us, on all Israel, and all the world, and let us say: Amen.

May the Source of peace send peace to all who mourn, and comfort to all who are bereaved. *Amen.*

At a House of Mourning

(One of the Weekday Services is read first)

We are assembled with our friends in the shadow that has fallen on their home. We raise our voices together in prayer to the Source of life, asking for comfort and strength.

We need light when gloom darkens our home; to whom shall we look, if not to the Creator of light? We need fortitude and courage when pain and loss assail us; where shall we find them, if not in the thought of the One who preserves all that is good from destruction?

Who among us has not passed through trials and bereavements? Some bear fresh wounds in their hearts, and therefore feel more keenly the kinship of sorrow; others, whose days of mourning are more remote, still recall the comfort that sympathy brought to their sorrowing hearts.

All things pass; all that lives must die. All that we prize is but lent to us, and the time comes when we must surrender it. We are travellers on the same road that leads to the same end.

MEDITATION

As in the world around us, so too in human life: darkness is followed by light, and sorrow by consolation. Life and death are twins; grief and hope walk hand in hand. Although we cannot know what lies beyond the body's death, we put our trust in the undying Spirit that calls us into life and abides to all eternity.

❖ ❖

Eternal God of the spirits of all flesh, You are close to the hearts of the sorrowing, to strengthen and console them with the warmth of Your love, and with the assurance that the human spirit is enduring and indestructible. Even as we pray for perfect peace for those whose lives have ended, so do we ask You to give comfort and courage to the living.

May the knowledge of Your nearness be our strength, O God, for You are with us at all times: in joy and sorrow, in light and darkness, in life and death.

אָנָּא, יי, הָרוֹפֵא לִשְׁבוּרֵי לֵב וּמְחַבֵּשׁ לְעַצְּבוֹתָם, שַׁלֵּם
נִחוּמִים לָאֲבֵלִים. חַזְּקֵם וְאַמְּצֵם בְּיוֹם אֶבְלָם וִיגוֹנָם,
וְזָכְרֵם לְחַיִּים טוֹבִים וַאֲרֻכִּים.
תֵּן בְּלִבָּם יִרְאָתְךָ וְאַהֲבָתְךָ לְעָבְדְךָ בְּלֵבָב שָׁלֵם.
וּתְהִי אַחֲרִיתָם שָׁלוֹם. אָמֵן.

O God, Healer of the broken-hearted and Binder of their wounds, grant consolation to those who mourn. Give them strength and courage in the time of their grief, and restore to them a sense of life's goodness.

Fill them with reverence and love, that they may serve You with a whole heart, and let them soon know peace. Amen.

Psalm 23

מִזְמוֹר לְדָוִד.
יהוה רֹעִי, לֹא אֶחְסָר. בִּנְאוֹת דֶּשֶׁא יַרְבִּיצֵנִי,
עַל־מֵי מְנֻחוֹת יְנַהֲלֵנִי. נַפְשִׁי יְשׁוֹבֵב,
יַנְחֵנִי בְמַעְגְּלֵי־צֶדֶק לְמַעַן שְׁמוֹ.
גַּם כִּי־אֵלֵךְ בְּגֵיא צַלְמָוֶת לֹא־אִירָא רָע,
כִּי־אַתָּה עִמָּדִי: שִׁבְטְךָ וּמִשְׁעַנְתֶּךָ, הֵמָּה יְנַחֲמֻנִי.
תַּעֲרֹךְ לְפָנַי שֻׁלְחָן נֶגֶד צֹרְרָי,
דִּשַּׁנְתָּ בַשֶּׁמֶן רֹאשִׁי, כּוֹסִי רְוָיָה.

אַךְ טוֹב וָחֶסֶד יִרְדְּפוּנִי כָּל־יְמֵי חַיָּי,
וְשַׁבְתִּי בְּבֵית־יהוה לְאֹרֶךְ יָמִים.

A Song of David.
Eternal God, You are my shepherd, I shall not want. You
make me lie down in green pastures, You lead me beside
still waters. You restore my soul; You guide me in paths of
righteousness for Your name's sake. Even when I walk
through the valley of the shadow of death, I will fear no
evil, for You are with me; with rod and staff You comfort
me. You prepare a table before me in the presence of my
enemies; You have anointed my head with oil; my cup is
overflowing. Surely, goodness and mercy shall follow me
all the days of my life, and I shall dwell in the house of the
Eternal God for ever.

❖ ❖

READ ONE OF THE FOLLOWING

At this hour, especially, the blessed presence of family and
friends brings us comfort and strength. It says to us: "Be sure
that love, the spring of life, abides."

May all who mourn take heart, as they remember the goodness
they have given and received. And when the days of their
mourning are ended, may the memory of their loved ones come
to be a benediction.

בָּרוּךְ אַתָּה יי, מְחַיֶּה הַכֹּל.

Ba-ruch a-ta Adonai, m'cha-yei ha-kol.

Praised be the Eternal Source of life.

90

❖ OR ❖

Psalm 121

אֶשָּׂא עֵינַי אֶל־הֶהָרִים: מֵאַיִן יָבֹא עֶזְרִי?

עֶזְרִי מֵעִם יהוה, עֹשֵׂה שָׁמַיִם וָאָרֶץ.

אַל־יִתֵּן לַמּוֹט רַגְלֶךָ, אַל־יָנוּם שֹׁמְרֶךָ.

הִנֵּה לֹא־יָנוּם וְלֹא יִישָׁן שׁוֹמֵר יִשְׂרָאֵל.

יהוה שֹׁמְרֶךָ, יהוה צִלְּךָ עַל־יַד יְמִינֶךָ.

יוֹמָם הַשֶּׁמֶשׁ לֹא־יַכֶּכָּה, וְיָרֵחַ בַּלָּיְלָה.

יהוה יִשְׁמָרְךָ מִכָּל־רָע, יִשְׁמֹר אֶת־נַפְשֶׁךָ.

יהוה יִשְׁמָר־צֵאתְךָ וּבוֹאֶךָ מֵעַתָּה וְעַד־עוֹלָם.

I lift my eyes to the mountains:
Where will I find my help?

> *My help will come from the Eternal One,*
> *Maker of heaven and earth,*

Your Guardian, who never slumbers,
will not let you fall.

> *Behold, the Guardian of Israel neither*
> *slumbers nor sleeps!*

The Eternal One is your Keeper, your shade at your side.
The sun shall not harm you by day, nor the moon by night.

The Eternal One will be your Shield against evil,
upholding your spirit.

The Eternal One will guard you, coming and going,
from this time forth and for ever.

❖ ❖

All rise

אֵל מָלֵא רַחֲמִים, שׁוֹכֵן בַּמְּרוֹמִים, הַמְצֵא מְנוּחָה נְכוֹנָה
תַּחַת כַּנְפֵי הַשְּׁכִינָה עִם קְדוֹשִׁים וּטְהוֹרִים כְּזֹהַר
הָרָקִיעַ מַזְהִירִים אֶת נִשְׁמַת . . . שֶׁהָלַךְ לְעוֹלָמוֹ
(שֶׁהָלְכָה לְעוֹלָמָהּ). בַּעַל הָרַחֲמִים יַסְתִּירֵהוּ (יַסְתִּירֶהָ)
בְּסֵתֶר כְּנָפָיו לְעוֹלָמִים. וְיִצְרוֹר בִּצְרוֹר הַחַיִּים אֶת־
נִשְׁמָתוֹ (נִשְׁמָתָהּ). יי הוּא נַחֲלָתוֹ (נַחֲלָתָהּ) וְיָנוּחַ
(וְתָנוּחַ) בְּשָׁלוֹם עַל מִשְׁכָּבוֹ (מִשְׁכָּבָהּ), וְנֹאמַר: אָמֵן.

God full of compassion, dwelling in the heights and in the
depths, grant perfect rest under the wings of Your Presence
to . . . , our loved one who has entered eternity. She/he has
found refuge for ever in the shadow of Your wings, and her/his
soul is bound up in the bond of eternal life; for You, the
Everlasting God, are her/his inheritance. May she/he rest in
peace, as we say: *Amen.*

Continue with Aleinu on page 74 or 77